TOP 55 Amazing and Simple Recipes in One Ketogenic Cookbook,

Any Recipes on Your Choice for Any Meal Time

D1707199

Get Your Free Bonus

I wanted to show my appreciation that you support my work so I've put together a bonus for you.

Keto Diet for Beginners:

Ketogenic Smoothie and Dessert Recipes

Just visit the link or scan QR-code to download it now:

https://goo.gl/qVCCVH

Thanks!

Amanda Lee

Table of Contents

Introduction

A vegetarian diet provides rewarding health benefits, but finding the right nutritional balance can be a bit challenging. Although meat and other non-vegetarian food products tend to be rich in nutrient content, it is possible to achieve a healthy and nutritional diet by consuming only vegetarian foods. Contrary to many meal charts that recommend meats and non-vegetarian products, this book will reveal the secrets to enjoying a strict yet robust vegetarian keto diet. To add to the challenge, many diet plans do not follow vegetarian standards by recommending a variety of non-vegetarian products. So, if you are tired of going through endless meal charts and finding that they do not suit your vegetarian lifestyle, we are here to help. We will explore many different vegetarian keto recipes in this book.

Ketogenic diets are gaining in prominence because they help people shed the extra pounds while maintaining muscle mass. This is possible because the diet causes one's body to burn fat as an energy source. With the help of ketogenic diet, one can gain the right body equilibrium and stay fit as well.

Rather than encouraging you to eat lots of meat like many other keto diets, we will be sticking to vegetarian recipes for you. So, if you do not know much about the ketogenic diet but you are looking for ways by which you could attain the right body mass index, here is what you need to know. In this book, we are going to give you comprehensive details about each and every aspect pertaining to the ketogenic diet and will prepare you to implement it in an apt manner.

Chapter 1: What Is A Vegetarian Ketogenic Diet?

A ketogenic diet is primarily a form of diet wherein the carb intake is restricted to ensure that the body enters a state of ketosis. Ketosis is the state wherein the body burns down stored units of fat as a source of energy. The energy which is broken down is used for carrying out the different body activities.

In a normal diet in which carbs are regularly consumed, the body is in a state of glycolysis, a process by which carbohydrates are broken down into glucose molecules which are used as energy. However, when the body enters a state of ketosis, as discussed above, fat molecules are used as energy, helping to rid the body of excess fat ensuring weight loss.

This controlled method of losing weight is much better than drastic means like crash dieting or even starving, as they have long-term negative side effects and likely will yield temporary results.

So, if you would like to stay fit, lose weight, and retain your muscle, you should definitely opt for the ketogenic diet.

Now, shifting our focus to the vegetarian ketogenic diet, the key difference here is that the recipes which we will share will all be vegetarian-based and won't include any kind of meat products whatsoever. The vegetarian ketogenic diet can be followed by both vegetarians and non-vegetarians. So, let us discuss some more details about the vegetarian ketogenic diet.

The Advantages of the Vegetarian Keto Diet Over Other Diets

When compared to most other diets, the vegetarian keto diet surely has many advantages to offer. Let us see the primary ones.

Systematic weight loss: This method of dieting leads to a systematic loss of weight. Do not expect to lose 10 kg in 10 days, but you will see your weight shedding systematically, and you are not likely to put it back again.

Muscular strength: Many forms of dieting are known to lead to loss of muscles as well. When you choose to opt for veg ketogenic diet, you will find that your muscular mass will be retained. You won't become lanky or feel lethargic because your muscles will still have the same kind of strength despite dieting.

You remain vegetarian: One of the best possible things about this diet is that for vegetarians, you do not have to alter your way of living. You still get your vegetarian options and still get to cut down your unwanted pounds without any trouble.

So, with these many possible advantages, it is definitely a recommended form of diet. Now that you have the incentives to opt for this diet form, let us explore more details.

The Types of Vegetarian Diet

It pays to know that even when it comes to vegetarian diet, there is a lot of variety with many sub-categories. Let us take a closer look at the possible vegetarian dieting forms.

Ideally, vegetarian diets can be categorized into four different classifications, and these include the following.

Lacto ovo vegetarians: These vegetarians eat both dairy products and eggs. It is the most common form of vegetarian diet. Neither eggs nor dairy are considered to be non-vegetarian, and this is why the meals under this diet form can include eggs and/or dairy products.

Lacto vegetarians: These vegetarians will eat dairy products, but they will refrain from including eggs in their meals.

Ovo vegetarians: These vegetarians will eat eggs, but they will refrain from including dairy in their meals.

Vegans: These vegetarians follow the strictest diet. They do not eat eggs or any dairy products. More broadly, they do not consume any food that is derived from an animal.

In this book, we are going to discuss **Lacto ovo** vegetarian meals. However, we'd like to draw your attention to the fact that lacto vegetarians, ovo vegetarians, and even vegans, followers of the strictest diet, also can use all the recipes presented in this book. Below, you'll see a table of lacto-ovo substitutions that can be used to replace a variety of dairy and egg ingredients.

Simply use these equivalent ingredients to customize our recipes to your individual vegetarian preferences. These substitutions will allow you to maintain your keto diet because the vegan-counterparts tend to contain even less carbs.

The Table of Keto-Friendly Vegan Replacements.

Ingredients		Serving size	Calories	Carbs	Total sugars in the carbs	Protein	Fat	Note
Egg, whole, middle		1 pcs	63 kcal	0.32 g	0.16 g	5.53 g	4.18 g	
Vegan Keto Replacement	Baking Soda and Vinegar	1 tbsp of baking soda + 1 tbsp of white vinegar	3 kcal	0.01 g	0.01 g	0 g	0 g	A decent egg replacement for fluffier baked goods.
	Silken Tofu	1/4 cup of pureed silken tofu	47 kcal	1.17 g	0.6 g	5.01 g	2.96 g	Silken tofu is a softer form of tofu that perfectly substitutes eggs. It is relatively flavorless but it can make baked goods dense, so it's best used in brownies and some quick breads and cakes.
	Ground Flax Seeds and water	1 tbsp of ground flax seeds + 3 tbsp of water	37 kcal	2.02 g	0.11 g	1.28 g	2.95 g	Finely ground flax makes an excellent binder. It has a nutty flavor that works best in recipes for almond or coconut flour baked goods and pancakes.
	The Neat Egg Natural Vegan Egg Substitute by Neat Foods	1 tbsp of neat egg mix + 2 tbsp of water	25 kcal	4 g	0 g	2 g	0 g	Perfect for baking. Vegan egg substitute that can be used in your favorite recipes as a binding agent in place of real eggs
	The Vegg Baking Mix	1 tsp + 1/4 cup water	10 kcal	1 g	0 g	2 g	0 g	It simulates the function and taste of eggs for baking. This powder works perfectly as a binding agent for all your baking needs. It is great for quiches, cakes, cookies, muffins, challah bread and much more.
	Follow Your Heart's VeganEgg	2 tbps + water	40 kcal	4 g	0 g	1 g	1.5 g	Great for baking cookies, muffins, cakes, and even for cooking up fluffy scrambled eggs and omelets
	The Vegg Tofu Scramble	4 tbsp + water	110 kcal	3 g	0 g	20 g	2 g	This "scrambled egg" mix gives you a high-protein way to enjoy your favorite breakfast foods.
Egg yolk, middle		1 pcs	48 kcal	0.2 g	0.09 g	2.4 g	3.9 g	
Vegan Keto Replacement	The Vegg Vegan Egg Yolk	1/2 tsp + 1/8 cup water	5 kcal	0.5 g	0 g	0.5 g	0 g	This is a 100% plant-based egg yolk replacement. It is great for french toast, dipping, hollandaise, and much more.

Ingredients		Serving size	Calories	Carbs	Total sugars in the carbs	Protein	Fat	Note
Butter		1 tbsp	102 kcal	0.01 g	0.01 g	0.12 g	11.52 g	
Vegan Keto Replacement	Coconut Oil	3/4 tbsp	88 kcal	0 g	0 g	0 g	10.2 g	Coconut oil has a slightly lower melting point than butter and the same smoke point as butter, which makes it a good butter replacement. Coconut oil is great for fat bombs, deserts, and cooking and baking at temperatures under 350 degrees Fahrenheit.
	Olive Oil	3/4 tbsp	89 kcal	0 g	0 g	0 g	10.1 g	You can use olive oil to enhance the flavor and fat content of the many dishes. Just make sure you cook with it at a temperature that is below 405 degrees Fahrenheit, so oil doesn't oxidize and become less healthy.
	Avocado Oil	3/4 tbsp	93 kcal	0 g	0 g	0 g	10.5 g	Avocado oil has the highest smoke point of any other cooking oil (at 520 degrees Fahrenheit), which makes it perfect for cooking, baking, and deep frying.
	Red Palm Oil	3/4 tbsp	90 kcal	0 g	0 g	0 g	11 g	Red palm oil has a mild carrot-like flavor and rich buttery texture. Also, it is a great source of A and E vitamins. Red palm oil is perfect to prepare vegan meats recipes and roast nuts and seeds at temperatures up to 450 degrees Fahrenheit

MCT Oil	3/4 tbsp	90 kcal	0 g	0 g	0 g	10.5 g	MCT oil contains medium-chain fats which are digested easily and sent directly to your liver where they are converted into ketones for fuel. Use this oil in fat bombs, salads, sauces and hot drinks when you need an energy boost.
Vegan Butter	1 tbsp	70-85 kcal	0 g	0 g	0 g	9-10 g	Make sure the vegan butter has no added sugars or hidden carbohydrates and it doesn't contain any hydrogenated oils because these oils increase the risk of heart disease tremendously.

Ingredients		Serving size	Calories	Carbs	Total sugars in the carbs	Protein	Fat	Note
Milk, 2% milkfat		1 cup	122 kcal	12 g	12 g	8 g	5 g	In recipes, you can substitute coconut milk in for regular milk in a 1 to 1 ratio. However, note that there are many varieties of coconut milk which contain different amounts of carbs, sugars, fats and proteins. Just make sure you choose the correct variant of coconut milk.
Milk, 3.25% milkfat		1 cup	149 kcal	12 g	12 g	8 g	8 g	
Vegan Keto Replacement	Coconut Milk	1 cup	45-550 kcal	1-15 g	0-8 g	1-5 g	4-57 g	
Heavy Cream		1 oz	98 kcal	0.8 g	0.8 g	0.6 g	10.5 g	Please, note that there are many varieties of coconut cream which contain different amounts of carbs, sugars, fats and proteins. Just make sure you choose the correct variant. You may have to blend in a bit of water or skim some water out of the container depending on the creaminess of the coconut cream.
Cream, light whipping		1 oz	83 kcal	0.84 g	0.84 g	0.62 g	8.8 g	
Vegan Keto Replacement	Coconut Cream	1 oz	15-95 kcal	1-2 g	0-0.5 g	0-1 g	5-10 g	
Cheese		1 oz	100-115 kcal	0-1 g	0-1 g	6-7 g	8-12 g	Please, note that there are many varieties of vegan cheese which contain different amounts of carbs, sugars, fats and proteins. Just make sure you choose the correct variant. If you want to avoid soy then you can find cashew, coconut or other tree-nut-based cheeses.
Vegan Keto Replacement	Vegan Cheese	1 oz	50-90 kcal	6-10 g	0 g	1-2 g	2-9 g	
Cream Cheese		1 oz	90-110 kcal	0-1 g	0-1 g	1-5 g	5-10 g	Please, note that there are many varieties of vegan cream cheese which contain different amounts of carbs, sugars, fats and proteins. Just make sure you choose the correct variant. If you want to avoid soy then you can find coconut, cashew, and other tree-nut-based cheeses.
Vegan Keto Replacement	Vegan Cream Cheese	1 oz	60-100 kcal	1-2 g	0 g	1-2 g	2-9 g	
Yogurt		1 cup	90-200 kcal	5-50 g	0-8 g	4-20 g	0-5 g	Please, note that there are very many varieties of vegan yogurt, and amounts of carbs, sugars, fats and proteins in these yogurts are very different. Please, make sure you choose the correct variant. You will probably be able to find plain almond, cashew, or coconut milk yogurt. Just make sure it does not contain excess carbs or sugars.
Vegan Keto Replacement	Vegan Yogurt	1 cup	50-400 kcal	2-20 g	0-2 g	4-12 g	0-50 g	
Sour Cream		1 cup	300-500 kcal	10-15 g	0-1 g	7-8 g	25-50 g	Please, note that there are many varieties of vegan sour cream which contain different amounts of carbs, sugars, fats and proteins.

Vegan Keto Replacement	Vegan Sour Cream	1 cup	400-900 kcal	15-25 g	0 g	1-6 g	40-90 g	Just make sure you choose the correct variant of vegan sour cream.

The Aspects of Vegetarian Ketogenic Diet

Let us see some of the core aspects pertaining to this form of ketogenic diet.

The tips First off, a word to the wise: prepare yourself for the keto flu. Many begin the dieting regiment with a great deal of excitement and enthusiasm, but within a week or two, it is likely that some not-so-exciting symptoms will develop. You may feel lethargic, have a mild headache, suffer from nausea, and even lose your appetite for anything and everything. This is what is known as the keto flu, and it is a common reaction your body undergoes when switching from carbs to fat as a source of energy. Stay strong and beat the flu and once the symptoms subside, you will be all set to follow the diet regiment again.

Be mindful of what you are eating. The ketogenic diet mainly aims at cutting down carb intake, but this doesn't mean that you can binge on fat products. You need to be sensible about what you are eating and be logical in your dieting pattern.

Follow the diet regiment thoroughly. It can be a little hard at the beginning, but with time, you should be able to follow it. So, despite the inevitable craving for carbs and high-fat foods, you should try to stay strong and curb the appetite for it. The results will help you in the long run.

The Incentives

Reduces the chance of heart disease

To give you even more incentive for the vegetarian ketogenic diet, let us give you a snapshot of the numerous benefits which you can reap simply from following this dieting pattern.

The keto diet has the potential to reduce the chances of heart disease. While this diet is known to lower the level of bad cholesterol in the body, it also improves the level of good cholesterol. Similarly, the diet can also cut down the level of triglycerides. So, all these cumulative changes are known to help in reducing the chances of heart disease.

Stabilizes the body's metabolism

The keto diet is also known to stabilize the metabolism of the body. While you might experience some taxing side-effects initially, your body will quickly adapt, and it won't be long before you inevitably begin to notice the benefits. Over time, your appetite will be molded by the keto diet regiment, and your body will naturally enter a state of metabolic stability.

Improved energy

The ketogenic diet is also known to result in an increase in energy levels as well. It is very common for people to feel much more energetic and to experience a significant improvement in their ability to focus. So, those who would like to increase their attention span should definitely consider following a vegetarian keto diet.

The Mistakes to Avoid

Now, let us see some of the common mistakes which you should try to avoid.

Do not give up.

No matter how hard it feels initially, stay committed to following the diet. After a week, your body will adjust to the new pattern, and this will help you follow the diet in a much easier way. So, you need to be committed to following the diet.

Do not binge eat.

The ketogenic diet doesn't mean that you can consume as much food as you want as long as it's not carbs. You need to understand the calories you are consuming and be systematic in your diet intake. Avoid carbs and also avoid all kinds of junk food as well.

Stay strong during the keto flu.

Be prepared to be hit by the keto flu and stay strong because this will give you a great head start in following the ketogenic diet. So even when the body feels a little down, stick to your diet, and the flu symptoms are likely to subside in a week or two.

Take care of your health.

Along with the keto diet, you should be mindful of your health. Try and add at least some minor workouts to your routine, such as a short jog, and it should help you stay fit much more easily.

Use these pointers and the positive changes will be apparent.

The Nutrients

Whenever you follow a ketogenic diet, it is important to be mindful of the nutrients. This means you should have an accurate picture of what to eat and what to avoid.

The food to restrict in the ketogenic vegetarian diet

Let us now give you details regarding which food you should exclude from your diet when choosing the vegetarian keto style of eating.

- All grains (even whole grain products) such as oats, barley, sorghum, and rice have to be avoided at all costs.
- You should also avoid things like sugar, honey, maple syrup, and agave as well.
- It's common knowledge that fruit is generally a healthy food choice, but following the keto vegetarian diet means that you need to steer clear of fruits like apple, oranges, and even bananas.
- Lentils, peas, and even black beans should also be avoided.
- Potatoes, yams, and related tubers are on the do-not-eat list as well.

The food to include in the keto vegetarian diet

Now, let us focus on the different foods you are allowed to eat while following this diet.

- Leafy green vegetables, like spinach and kale, are a good choice.
- Vegetables that are grown above ground, like cauliflower, zucchini, and even broccoli, are good options.
- Tempeh, seitan tofu, and any high-protein, low-carb food products are a great addition to a meal.
- Try to include nuts and seeds in your diet. Pumpkin seeds, sunflower seeds, almonds, and pistachios are just a few flavorful options.
- If you're feeling adventurous, try to cook with sea vegetables, such as bladderwrack or kelp.
- Feel free to add fermented foods, like sauerkraut and kimchi, to your meals.
- Foods which have a low glycemic index, including avocado, blackberries, and raspberries, can serve as a nutritious and flavorful addition to your keto vegetarian diet.

So, these are some of the elementary details regarding the ketogenic diet. With these many details, you should now have a very clear picture pertaining to how this whole diet works.

Many people have been following the keto diet for decades now, and there is no mistake that the results are clear and easy to witness. They not only managed to get rid of the extra pounds, but at the same time, they have greatly improved their overall health.

One of the key things which you need to remember when following the veg ketogenic diet is to be the fact that you must follow a systematic and disciplined approach. Your inability to do so would surely hamper the benefits that you would otherwise reap from this diet.

While you have many of the details now, you must be wondering about the possible meals you can cook. We do know that following a strictly vegetarian diet cuts down on many options, and this is why we are going to give you precise recipes which you can follow when making your own meals. With these meals, you will be able to successfully follow the ketogenic diet and observe the changes in your body as well.

Chapter 2: Recipes

In this chapter, we are going to share some of the best recipes with you which will help you prepare scrumptious vegetarian meals that are sure to satiate your appetite and serve your health goals as well. We will make it a point to split the recipes into breakfast, snacks, lunch, and dinner categories so that you will have plenty of meal options throughout the day.

All these meals are vegetarian, and they should all be easy to follow.

Vegetarian Ketogenic Breakfast Recipes

1. Vegetarian Keto Club Salad

This is the recipe for the right kind of salad which can be the perfect kick-start to your day.

Ingredients

- 3 large hard-boiled eggs, sliced
- 3 cups romaine lettuce, shredded into pieces
- 1 cup diced cucumber
- ½ cup of halved cherry tomatoes
- 4 ounces cubed cheddar cheese
- ½ tsp onion powder
- 1 tbsp Dijon mustard
- 1 tbsp milk
- 2 tbsp sour cream
- ½ tsp garlic powder
- 1 tsp dried parsley
- 2 tbsp mayonnaise

Instructions

- In a small bowl, mix sour cream, mayonnaise, onion powder, garlic powder, and dried parsley thoroughly until combined completely.
- Now, add 1 tbsp of milk and mix well.
- If you feel that the mixture is quite thick, you may add one more tbsp of milk.
- In a separate medium bowl, layer the salad with romaine lettuce, cucumber, tomatoes, sliced egg, and cheddar cheese.
- Add a tablespoon of Dijon mustard to the center of the salad.
- Drizzle dressing on top of salad, and toss to coat.
- Serve.

GENERAL		
Servings quantity: 2		
Weight:	Total = 683.00 g	Per one serving = 341.50 g

Mass fraction:	Percentagewise	Total	Per 1 serving
Protein:	7.59 %	51.81 g	25.91 g
Fat:	11.61 %	79.27 g	39.64 g
Carbohydrates:	2.77 %	18.94 g	9.47 g

CALORIE BREAKDOWN			
Energy (calories):	Total = 993.00 kcal	Per one serving = 496.50 kcal	
Calorie breakdown:	Percentagewise	Total	Per 1 serving
Protein:	21 %	209.00 kcal	104.50 kcal
Fat:	72 %	713.00 kcal	356.50 kcal
Carbohydrates:	7 %	71.00 kcal	35.50 kcal

CARBOHYDRATES				
	Per cent of total carbohydrates mass	Per cent of total weight	Total	Per 1 serving
Total Carbohydrates:		2.77 %	18.94 g	9.47 g
Dietary Fiber:	30.10 %	0.83 %	5.70 g	2.85 g
Sugars(net carbs):	**44.93 %**	**1.25 %**	**8.51 g**	**4.26 g**

2. Keto Brownie Muffins

Aren't muffins the best way to start your day? Let us see the right way to prepare them perfectly.

Ingredients

- 1 large egg
- ½ cup pumpkin puree
- ¼ cup slivered almonds
- 1 cup of golden flaxseed meal
- ½ tbsp baking powder
- ¼ cup cocoa powder
- ¼ cup sugar-free caramel syrup
- 2 tbsp coconut oil
- 1 tsp apple cider vinegar
- 1 tbsp cinnamon
- ½ tsp salt
- 1 tsp vanilla extract

Instructions

- Preheat the oven to 350 °F.
- In a mixing bowl, add all dry ingredients (except for slivered almonds), and mix well to combine.
- In a separate bowl, add all wet ingredients, and mix well.
- Now, pour the wet ingredients into the bowl with the dry ingredients, and once again mix it thoroughly.
- Add paper liners to a muffin tin, and then add ¼ cup of batter into each liner.
- Now, sprinkle some slivered almonds over the batter of each muffin liner, and gently press them into the batter to ensure that they stick.
- Bake for about 15 minutes.
- Serve.

GENERAL			
Servings quantity: 6			
Weight:	Total = 565.00 g	Per one serving = 94.17 g	
Mass fraction:	Percentagewise	Total	Per 1 serving
Protein:	10.60 %	59.88 g	9.98 g
Fat:	25.51 %	144.14 g	24.02 g
Carbohydrates:	18.73 %	105.83 g	17.64 g

CALORIE BREAKDOWN			
Energy (calories):	Total = 1782.00 kcal	Per one serving = 297.00 kcal	
Calorie breakdown:	Percentagewise	Total	Per 1 serving
Protein:	12 %	206.00 kcal	34.33 kcal
Fat:	68 %	1217.00 kcal	202.83 kcal
Carbohydrates:	20 %	359.00 kcal	59.83 kcal

CARBOHYDRATES

	Per cent of total carbohydrates mass	Per cent of total weight	Total	Per 1 serving
Total Carbohydrates:		18.73 %	105.83 g	17.64 g
Dietary Fiber:	72.38 %	13.56 %	76.60 g	12.77 g
Sugars(net carbs):	8.46 %	**1.58 %**	**8.95 g**	**1.49 g**

3. Crispy Tofu and Bok Choy Salad

Yet another delectable salad option, this one surely makes a great breakfast.

Ingredients

For the oven baked tofu

- 15 ounces extra firm tofu
- 1 tbsp rice wine vinegar
- 1 tbsp sesame oil
- 1 tbsp soy sauce
- 2 tsp minced garlic
- Juice of ½ lemon
- 1 tbsp water

For the bok choy salad

- 9 ounces bok choy
- 1 tbsp sambal olek
- 2 tbsp chopped cilantro
- 1 stalk green onion
- 1 tbsp peanut butter
- 7 drops liquid stevia
- 3 tbsp coconut oil
- 2 tbsp soy sauce
- Juice of ½ lime

Instructions

- Lay out a kitchen towel and layer the tofu over half of it. Fold the towel over the tofu, and press to dry the tofu. If possible, place something heavy on top of the folded towel to keep the tofu pressed. It will take almost 6 hours to dry completely, and you may even have to change the towel halfway.
- In a bowl, add soy sauce, garlic, lemon juice, sesame oil, and vinegar and mix well. This will be the tofu marinade.
- After the tofu is dried, chop it evenly into square pieces. Add it to a plastic bag along with the marinade.
- Let the tofu marinate for nearly 30 minutes. You can also keep it overnight for even more flavor.
- Now preheat the oven to 350 °F, line a baking sheet with parchment paper, and bake the marinated tofu on the baking sheet for 30 minutes.
- Now, we will work on the bok choy salad. For this, you need to first chop the green onion and the cilantro.
- Add all remaining bok choy salad ingredients apart from bok choy and lime juice in a separate bowl and mix well.
- Now, add the chopped green onion and cilantro to it.
- When the tofu has been cooked thoroughly, add lime juice to the salad bowl and mix well.

- Now, chop the bok choy.
- Add the tofu and the chopped bok choy to the salad bowl and mix.
- Serve.

GENERAL			
Servings quantity: 4			
Weight:	Total = 930.00 g	Per one serving = 232.50 g	
Mass fraction:	Percentagewise	Total	Per 1 serving
Protein:	6.05 %	56.29 g	14.07 g
Fat:	9.46 %	88.02 g	22.01 g
Carbohydrates:	2.89 %	26.85 g	6.71 g

CALORIE BREAKDOWN			
Energy (calories):	Total = 1046.00 kcal	Per one serving = 261.50 kcal	
Calorie breakdown:	Percentagewise	Total	Per 1 serving
Protein:	18 %	191.00 kcal	47.75 kcal
Fat:	72 %	753.00 kcal	188.25 kcal
Carbohydrates:	10 %	101.00 kcal	25.25 kcal

CARBOHYDRATES				
	Per cent of total carbohydrates mass	Per cent of total weight	Total	Per 1 serving
Total Carbohydrates:		2.89 %	26.85 g	6.71 g
Dietary Fiber:	23.84 %	0.69 %	6.40 g	1.60 g
Sugars(net carbs):	33.82 %	0.98 %	9.08 g	2.27 g

4. Grilled Cheese Sandwich

For the sandwich lovers out there, this surely is a great way to have breakfast. Easy to make, it is a great recipe which surely fills the appetite.

Ingredients
- 2 large eggs
- 1 ½ tbsp psyllium husk powder
- 2 tbsp soft butter
- 2 tbsp almond flour
- ½ tsp baking powder
- Several slices of your choice of cheese
- An additional 1 tbsp of butter

Instructions
- Put 2 tbsp of butter in a bowl, and let it come to room temperature. When it has turned soft, add 2 tbsp of almond flour and again 1 ½ tbsp of psyllium husk to it.
- Also add ½ tsp of baking powder. Mix everything well until you get a thick dough.
- Now add 2 large eggs and mix well.
- Now, microwave the dough for about 100 seconds.
- Now, let it settle and then tap at the bottom. Cut it into two halves.
- Measure the amount of cheese you need and then stick it in between the two dough halves, which serve as your sandwich buns.
- Add the additional 1 tbsp of butter to a pan. Put the pan on medium heat. When the pan has turned hot, add the dough with cheese, and then cook on both sides.
- Serve it with a side salad.

GENERAL			
Servings quantity: 1			
Weight:	Total = 226.50 g	Per one serving = 226.50 g	
Mass fraction:	Percentagewise	Total	Per 1 serving
Protein:	12.80 %	29.00 g	29.00 g
Fat:	30.44 %	68.95 g	68.95 g
Carbohydrates:	8.27 %	18.73 g	18.73 g

CALORIE BREAKDOWN			
Energy (calories):	Total = 801.00 kcal	Per one serving = 801.00 kcal	
Calorie breakdown:	Percentagewise	Total	Per 1 serving
Protein:	15 %	119.00 kcal	119.00 kcal
Fat:	76 %	610.00 kcal	610.00 kcal
Carbohydrates:	9 %	73.00 kcal	73.00 kcal

CARBOHYDRATES				
	Per cent of total carbohydrates mass	Per cent of total weight	Total	Per 1 serving
Total Carbohydrates:		8.27 %	18.73 g	18.73 g
Dietary Fiber:	80.09 %	6.62 %	15.00 g	15.00 g
Sugars(net carbs):	5.71 %	**0.47 %**	**1.07 g**	**1.07 g**

5. Sun-Dried Tomato Pesto Mug Cake

A sweet start to your day, this is a quick fix for breakfast.

Ingredients

For the base

- 1 large egg
- ½ tsp of baking powder
- 2 tbsp of almond flour
- 2 tbsp of butter

For the flavor

- 1 tbsp almond flour
- 5 tsp of sun-dried tomato pesto
- A pinch of salt

Instructions

- Add all the ingredients to a microwave-safe mug, and mix well.
- Microwave it for 75 seconds on high power.
- Now, slam the mug against a plate to help loosen the cake from the mug.
- Add extra tomato pesto to it if desired, and serve.

GENERAL			
Servings quantity: 1			
Weight:	Total = 105.00 g	Per one serving = 105.00 g	
Mass fraction:	Percentagewise	Total	Per 1 serving
Protein:	8.44 %	8.86 g	8.86 g
Fat:	31.96 %	33.56 g	33.56 g
Carbohydrates:	5.73 %	6.02 g	6.02 g

CALORIE BREAKDOWN			
Energy (calories):	Total = 350.00 kcal	Per one serving = 350.00 kcal	
Calorie breakdown:	Percentagewise	Total	Per 1 serving
Protein:	10 %	36.00 kcal	36.00 kcal
Fat:	84 %	294.00 kcal	294.00 kcal
Carbohydrates:	6 %	21.00 kcal	21.00 kcal

CARBOHYDRATES				
	Per cent of total carbohydrates mass	Per cent of total weight	Total	Per 1 serving
Total Carbohydrates:		5.73 %	6.02 g	6.02 g
Dietary Fiber:	29.90 %	1.71 %	1.80 g	1.80 g
Sugars(net carbs):	9.30 %	0.53 %	0.56 g	0.56 g

6. Cheesy Thyme Waffles

A lot of us enjoy waffles as a great start to our day. If you are ready to prepare one, here is a quick recipe for it.

Ingredients

- 2 stalks green onion
- ½ riced large head of cauliflower
- 2 large eggs
- 2 tsp of fresh chopped thyme
- 1 cup finely shredded mozzarella cheese
- 1 tbsp of sesame seeds
- 1 cup of packed collard greens
- 1/3 cup parmesan cheese
- 1 tsp of garlic powder
- 1 tbsp of olive oil
- ½ tsp salt
- ½ tsp of ground black pepper

Instructions

- Cut the cauliflower into small florets and slice the green onions as well. Now rip the thyme off the stems.
- Add cauliflower to a food processor, and churn until it is thoroughly processed. Add green onions, collard greens, and thyme to the food processor, and pulse everything again.
- Now add the processed mixture to a large mixing bowl.
- To the large bowl, also add a cup of mozzarella cheese along with the eggs, the sesame seeds, olive oil, parmesan cheese, black pepper, salt, and garlic powder.
- Mix well to form a smooth batter. Now heat the waffle iron and have it ready.
- Pour the mixture into the waffle iron, ensuring it is spread evenly.
- Cook it well and serve hot.

GENERAL			
Servings quantity: 8			
Weight:	Total = 756.00 g	Per one serving = 94.50 g	
Mass fraction:	Percentagewise	Total	Per 1 serving
Protein:	7.74 %	58.48 g	7.31 g
Fat:	8.37 %	63.30 g	7.91 g
Carbohydrates:	4.96 %	37.49 g	4.69 g

CALORIE BREAKDOWN			
Energy (calories):	Total = 926.00 kcal	Per one serving = 115.75 kcal	
Calorie breakdown:	Percentagewise	Total	Per 1 serving
Protein:	25 %	231.00 kcal	28.88 kcal
Fat:	60 %	557.00 kcal	69.63 kcal
Carbohydrates:	15 %	137.00 kcal	17.13 kcal

CARBOHYDRATES			
	Per cent of total carbohydrates mass	Per cent of total weight	Total	Per 1 serving

Total Carbohydrates:		4.96 %	37.49 g	4.69 g
Dietary Fiber:	32.28 %	1.60 %	12.10 g	1.51 g
Sugars(net carbs):	28.75 %	**1.43 %**	**10.78 g**	**1.35 g**

7. Warm Asian Broccoli Salad

As salads make for a quick and easy breakfast option, here is how you can have this one ready.

Ingredients

- 12 ounce bag broccoli slaw
- ½ cup full-fat plain goat milk yogurt
- 1 tsp fresh ginger, grated
- 2 tbsp coconut oil
- 1 tbsp coconut amines
- ½ tbsp sesame seeds
- ½ tsp salt
- ¼ tsp pepper
- Cilantro as garnish, optional

Instructions

- Add the coconut oil to a large skillet, and heat over medium-high flame.
- Now add the broccoli slaw to the skillet.
- Cover and cook for about 7 minutes.
- Now, remove cover and mix in the ginger, coconut amines, salt, and pepper.
- Remove the skillet from heat, and add the yogurt along with the sesame seeds.
- Garnish with cilantro, if you desire.
- Serve.

GENERAL			
Servings quantity: 2			
Weight:	Total = 511.00 g	Per one serving = 255.50 g	
Mass fraction:	Percentagewise	Total	Per 1 serving
Protein:	3.36 %	17.15 g	8.58 g
Fat:	6.55 %	33.45 g	16.73 g
Carbohydrates:	6.75 %	34.50 g	17.25 g

CALORIE BREAKDOWN			
Energy (calories):	Total = 449.00 kcal	Per one serving = 224.50 kcal	
Calorie breakdown:	Percentagewise	Total	Per 1 serving
Protein:	11 %	49.80 kcal	24.90 kcal
Fat:	64 %	288.00 kcal	144.00 kcal
Carbohydrates:	28 %	126.20 kcal	63.10 kcal

CARBOHYDRATES				
	Per cent of total carbohydrates mass	Per cent of total weight	Total	Per 1 serving
Total Carbohydrates:		6.75 %	34.50 g	17.25 g
Dietary Fiber:	36.81 %	2.49 %	12.70 g	6.35 g
Sugars(net carbs):	60.17 %	**4.06 %**	**20.76 g**	**10.38 g**

8. Vegan Keto Porridge

This amazingly delicious porridge is apt for breakfast.

Ingredients

- 2 tbsp of coconut flour
- 2 tbsp of vanilla protein powder; vegan
- 1 tsp of powdered erythritol
- 3 tbsp of golden flaxseed meal
- 1 ½ cups of unsweetened almond milk

Instructions

- In a bowl, mix golden flaxseed meal along with coconut flour and protein powder.
- Add this mixture to a saucepan. Add the almond milk, and cook over medium heat.
- When it begins to thicken, add the desired amount of erythritol (sweetener).
- Serve it with your favorite toppings.

GENERAL			
Servings quantity: 1			
Weight:	Total = 421.00 g	Per one serving = 421.00 g	
Mass fraction:	Percentagewise	Total	Per 1 serving
Protein:	4.79 %	20.16 g	20.16 g
Fat:	5.74 %	24.15 g	24.15 g
Carbohydrates:	3.86 %	16.24 g	16.24 g

CALORIE BREAKDOWN			
Energy (calories):	Total = 340.00 kcal	Per one serving = 340.00 kcal	
Calorie breakdown:	Percentagewise	Total	Per 1 serving
Protein:	30 %	100.36 kcal	100.36 kcal
Fat:	58 %	198.29 kcal	198.29 kcal
Carbohydrates:	12 %	41.34 kcal	41.34 kcal

CARBOHYDRATES				
	Per cent of total carbohydrates mass	Per cent of total weight	Total	Per 1 serving
Total Carbohydrates:		3.86 %	16.24 g	16.24 g
Dietary Fiber:	57.39 %	2.21 %	9.32 g	9.32 g
Sugars(net carbs):	12.38 %	**0.48 %**	**2.01**	**2.01**

9. Keto Cashew Yogurt Sundae

This is one of the best breakfasts to make when you have guests coming over and you want to keep it healthy.

Ingredients for the Keto Cashew Yogurt

- 1½ cup of boiling water
- ½ cup raw cashews
- 1 tbs erythritol
- 1 tbsp lemon juice

Instructions

- Put cashews in a heat safe bowl.
- Boil water, and slowly pour over cashew.
- Add the erythritol and lemon juice to the bowl, stir until the erythritol is well dissolved.
- Make sure your blender can handle hot liquids and carefully put everything in a blender.
- Blend until the cashews are nice and smooth, and the mixture has thickened.
- Let the mixture cool for about ten-fifteen minutes, then chill it in the fridge for about a few hours.
- Serve.

Here are the nutrient facts of the Keto Cashew Yogurt:

GENERAL			
Servings quantity: 3 servings for sundae (each serving is about 2/3 cup)			
Weight:	Total = 437.50 g	Per one serving = 145.83 g	
Mass fraction:	Percentagewise	Total	Per 1 serving
Protein:	2.61 %	11.44 g	3.81 g
Fat:	6.27 %	27.45 g	9.15 g
Carbohydrates:	5.47 %	23.92 g	7.97 g

CALORIE BREAKDOWN			
Energy (calories):	Total = 349.00 kcal	Per one serving = 116.33 kcal	
Calorie breakdown:	Percentagewise	Total	Per 1 serving
Protein:	11 %	39.50 kcal	13.17 kcal
Fat:	66 %	229.50 kcal	76.50 kcal
Carbohydrates:	23 %	79.50 kcal	26.50 kcal

CARBOHYDRATES				
	Per cent of total carbohydrates mass	Per cent of total weight	Total	Per 1 serving
Total Carbohydrates:		5.47 %	23.92 g	7.97 g
Dietary Fiber:	17.14 %	0.94 %	4.10 g	1.37 g
Sugars(net carbs):	17.06 %	**0.93 %**	**4.08 g**	**1.36 g**

Ingredients for the Keto Cashew Yogurt Sundae
- 2/3 cup of cashew yogurt; low carb and vegan
- ¼ cup of frozen berries
- 1 tbsp of hemp seeds
- 1 tbsp of flax and chia blend

Instructions
- All you need to do is take all of the ingredients and mix together in whichever manner you deem appropriate.
- Serve.

Table of Keto Berries Nutrition Facts:

| Berries | Energy (calories), kcal | Weight, g | Mass fraction, g | | | | |
			Fat	Protein	Carbo-hydrates	Fiber	Sugars (net carbs)
Raspberries, frozen, ¼ cup	18.25	35.00	0.23	0.42	4.18	2.28	1.55
Blueberries, frozen, ¼ cup	19.75	38.75	0.25	0.16	4.72	1.05	3.28
Strawberries, frozen, ¼ cup	13.00	37.25	0.04	0.16	3.40	0.78	1.70
Blackberries, frozen, ¼ cup	24.25	37.75	0.16	0.45	5.92	1.90	4.03

Nutrition facts of the Keto Cashew Yogurt Sundae, when using raspberries:

GENERAL			
Servings quantity: 1			
Weight:	Total = 200.88 g	Per one serving = 200.88 g	
Mass fraction:	Percentagewise	Total	Per 1 serving
Protein:	4.58 %	9.20 g	9.20 g
Fat:	8.11 %	16.28 g	16.28 g
Carbohydrates:	8.00 %	16.07 g	16.07 g

CALORIE BREAKDOWN			
Energy (calories):	Total = 213.42 kcal	Per one serving = 213.42 kcal	
Calorie breakdown:	Percentagewise	Total	Per 1 serving
Protein:	22 %	47.54 kcal	47.54 kcal
Fat:	58 %	124.74 kcal	124.74 kcal
Carbohydrates:	19 %	40.99 kcal	40.99 kcal

CARBOHYDRATES			
	Per cent of total carbohydrates mass	Per cent of total weight	Total	Per 1 serving
Total Carbohydrates:		8.00 %	16.07 g	16.07 g
Dietary Fiber:	43.35 %	3.47 %	6.97 g	6.97 g
Sugars(net carbs):	18.00 %	1.44 %	2.89 g	2.89

10. Keto Cereal

This keto cereal is a healthy choice for anyone who is looking to shed extra pounds without compromising taste.

Ingredients
- ½ cup of shredded coconut
- 2 cups of almond milk
- 1/3 cup of crushed walnut pieces
- 1/3 cup of toasted flaxseed
- 3 to 4 tsp of butter
- 2 tsp of erythritol or sweetener of your choice
- 1 tsp of salt

Instructions
- Melt the butter on medium heat.
- Add the walnut pieces, flaxseed, and salt to the melted butter and stir for a couple of minutes.
- Add shredded coconut and keep mixing. Make sure the bottom doesn't start to burn.
- To this mixture, add the sweetener of your choice. Ideally, it shouldn't be more than 1 tbsp.
- Now, quickly add your milk.
- Stir and turn off the heat.

Note: Do not add too many nuts as it might defeat the purpose of following a ketogenic diet.

GENERAL			
Servings quantity: 2			
Weight:	Total = 645.00 g	Per one serving = 322.50 g	
Mass fraction:	Percentagewise	Total	Per 1 serving
Protein:	3.02 %	19.48 g	9.74 g
Fat:	12.62 %	81.39 g	40.70 g
Carbohydrates:	5.49 %	35.39 g	17.70 g

CALORIE BREAKDOWN			
Energy (calories):	Total = 879.00 kcal	Per one serving = 439.50 kcal	
Calorie breakdown:	Percentagewise	Total	Per 1 serving
Protein:	9 %	78.50 kcal	39.25 kcal
Fat:	78 %	689.50 kcal	344.75 kcal
Carbohydrates:	13 %	111.00 kcal	55.50 kcal

CARBOHYDRATES				
	Per cent of total carbohydrates mass	Per cent of total weight	Total	Per 1 serving
Total Carbohydrates:		5.49 %	35.39 g	17.70 g
Dietary Fiber:	60.19 %	3.30 %	21.30 g	10.65 g
Sugars(net carbs):	12.35 %	**0.68 %**	**4.37 g**	**2.19 g**

11. Keto Bagel

Bagels are always a satisfying choice. Not your average bagel, this recipe will definitely help you with a healthy and tasty start to your day.

Ingredients

- ½ cup hemp hearts
- ¼ cup psyllium fibre
- 6 egg whites, organic
- 1 cup coconut flour
- ½ cup sesame seed kernels
- ½ cup pumpkin seeds
- 1 tbsp baking powder
- 1 tsp Celtic sea salt
- 1 cup boiling water

Instructions

- Preheat the oven to 350 °F.
- Mix all the ingredients except the eggs and sesame seeds in a large bowl.
- Blend the egg whites in a blender until you get a foamy mixture.
- Pour the egg whites into the well-churned dry ingredients and mix until smooth.
- Add a cup of boiling water and keep stirring until a smooth dough forms.
- Now place parchment paper on a cookie sheet.
- Divide the dough into 6 balls of roughly equal size.
- With your finger, make a hole in each ball then press the dough onto the cookie sheet, forming it in the shape of a bagel.
- Sprinkle the sesame seeds on top.
- Bake them for 55 minutes at 350 °F.

GENERAL			
Servings quantity: 6 (6 bagels)			
Weight:	Total = 575.00 g	Per one serving = 95.83 g	
Mass fraction:	Percentagewise	Total	Per 1 serving
Protein:	16.77 %	96.43 g	16.07 g
Fat:	21.82 %	125.49 g	20.92 g
Carbohydrates:	20.21 %	116.19 g	19.37 g

CALORIE BREAKDOWN			
Energy (calories):	Total = 1791.00 kcal	Per one serving = 298.50 kcal	
Calorie breakdown:	Percentagewise	Total	Per 1 serving
Protein:	22 %	387.20 kcal	64.53 kcal
Fat:	53 %	941.80 kcal	156.97 kcal
Carbohydrates:	26 %	462.00 kcal	77.00 kcal

CARBOHYDRATES				
	Per cent of total carbohydrates mass	Per cent of total weight	Total	Per 1 serving
Total Carbohydrates:		20.21 %	116.19 g	19.37 g
Dietary Fiber:	69.63 %	14.07 %	80.90 g	13.48 g
Sugars(net carbs):	9.18 %	**1.86 %**	**10.67 g**	**1.78 g**

12. Green Low Carb Breakfast Smoothie

For those who love smoothies, this low carb treat offers something delicious to sip on while keeping you on your keto diet.

Ingredients

- 1 oz of spinach
- 2 oz of celery
- 1 ½ cups of almond milk
- 2 oz avocado
- 2 oz of cucumber
- 1 tbsp coconut oil
- 1 scoop of protein powder
- 10 drops of liquid stevia
- ½ tsp of chia seeds

Instructions

- Add almond milk and spinach to blender.
- Blend briefly.
- Add the rest of the ingredients (except chia seeds) to the slightly blended mixture and blend thoroughly.
- Pour mixture into a glass and sprinkle chia seeds on top.

GENERAL			
Servings quantity: 2			
Weight:	Total = 613.76 g	Per one serving = 306.88 g	
Mass fraction:	Percentagewise	Total	Per 1 serving
Protein:	4.68 %	28.70 g	14.35 g
Fat:	4.74 %	29.10 g	14.55 g
Carbohydrates:	2.59 %	15.87 g	7.94 g

CALORIE BREAKDOWN			
Energy (calories):	Total = 429.50 kcal	Per one serving = 214.75 kcal	
Calorie breakdown:	Percentagewise	Total	Per 1 serving
Protein:	29 %	125.42 kcal	62.71 kcal
Fat:	57 %	242.77 kcal	121.38 kcal
Carbohydrates:	14 %	61.31 kcal	30.66 kcal

CARBOHYDRATES				
	Per cent of total carbohydrates mass	Per cent of total weight	Total	Per 1 serving
Total Carbohydrates:		2.59 %	15.87 g	7.94 g
Dietary Fiber:	41.59 %	1.08 %	6.60 g	3.30 g
Sugars(net carbs):	32.77 %	**0.85 %**	**5.20 g**	**2.60 g**

13. Hot Blueberry Coconut Cereal

Coconut is always a good choice when it comes to breakfast. It satisfies your appetite without piling on too many carbs.

Ingredients

For the cereal
- ¼ cup of coconut flour
- 1 cup of almond milk
- 10 drops of liquid stevia
- ¼ cup of ground flaxseed
- 1 tsp of vanilla extract
- A pinch of salt
- A pinch of cinnamon

Toppings
- 2 oz of blueberries
- 1 oz of shaved coconut
- 2 tbsp of butter
- 2 tbsp of pumpkin seeds

Instructions
- Pour almond milk into a small pot and heat on low.
- Add flaxseed, coconut flour, salt, and cinnamon. Whisk the mixture gently.
- Slowly increase heat until it starts to bubble. Then, add vanilla extract and liquid stevia, and stir.
- When the mixture has thickened, turn off heat and add toppings.

GENERAL			
Servings quantity: 2			
Weight:	Total = 444.76 g	Per one serving = 222.38 g	
Mass fraction:	Percentagewise	Total	Per 1 serving
Protein:	3.76 %	16.72 g	8.36 g
Fat:	13.37 %	59.48 g	29.74 g
Carbohydrates:	9.29 %	41.32 g	20.66 g

CALORIE BREAKDOWN			
Energy (calories):	Total = 750.50 kcal	Per one serving = 375.25 kcal	
Calorie breakdown:	Percentagewise	Total	Per 1 serving
Protein:	9 %	66.30 kcal	33.15 kcal
Fat:	68 %	512.20 kcal	256.10 kcal
Carbohydrates:	22 %	162.00 kcal	81.00 kcal

CARBOHYDRATES				
	Per cent of total carbohydrates mass	Per cent of total weight	Total	Per 1 serving
Total Carbohydrates:		9.29 %	41.32 g	20.66 g
Dietary Fiber:	58.45 %	5.43 %	24.15 g	12.08 g
Sugars(net carbs):	25.88 %	2.40 %	10.70 g	5.35 g

14. Coconut Macadamia Bars

If you're looking for something different, try these coconut macadamia bars. Easy to cook, they're ready in as little as 10 minutes.

Ingredients

- 4 oz of macadamia nuts
- 1/2 cup of coconut oil
- 40 drops of stevia
- 12 tbsp of unsweetened shredded coconut

Instructions

- Crush the macadamia nuts thoroughly in a blender.
- In a mixing bowl, add coconut oil and shredded coconut. Mix thoroughly.
- Add the macadamia nuts and stevia drops.
- Mix thoroughly, and then pour the batter into a 9x9 baking dish lined with parchment paper.
- Refrigerate the mixture overnight.
- Cut into 9 pieces and serve.

Note: If you want crunchier bars, store them in the freezer.

GENERAL			
Servings quantity: 9 (each serving is about 1 $^1/_3$ ounces)			
Weight:	Total = 333.04 g	Per one serving = 37.00 g	
Mass fraction:	Percentagewise	Total	Per 1 serving
Protein:	3.45 %	11.50 g	1.28 g
Fat:	66.17 %	220.38 g	24.49 g
Carbohydrates:	8.18 %	27.24 g	3.03 g

CALORIE BREAKDOWN			
Energy (calories):	Total = 2022.00 kcal	Per one serving = 224.67 kcal	
Calorie breakdown:	Percentagewise	Total	Per 1 serving
Protein:	2 %	40.00 kcal	4.44 kcal
Fat:	93 %	1872.00 kcal	208.00 kcal
Carbohydrates:	5 %	110.00 kcal	12.22 kcal

CARBOHYDRATES				
	Per cent of total carbohydrates mass	Per cent of total weight	Total	Per 1 serving
Total Carbohydrates:		8.18 %	27.24 g	3.03 g
Dietary Fiber:	60.94 %	4.98 %	16.60 g	1.84 g
Sugars(net carbs):	36.42 %	2.98 %	9.92 g	1.10 g

15. Tofu Scramble

This is another quick-to-make breakfast which you can munch on when you have a long day at work.

Ingredients

- 1 block of tofu, extra firm
- ½ cup of cherry tomatoes
- ½ cup of spinach, frozen
- 1 tbsp of olive oil
- Garlic powder
- Onion powder
- Salt and pepper to taste

Instructions

- Dice tofu and cut tomatoes into halves; in a bowl, mix together all of the ingredients.
- Sauté mixture on skillet.
- Serve.

GENERAL			
Servings quantity: 2			
Weight:	Total = 621.00 g	Per one serving = 310.50 g	
Mass fraction:	Percentagewise	Total	Per 1 serving
Protein:	7.81 %	48.49 g	24.25 g
Fat:	6.54 %	40.62 g	20.31 g
Carbohydrates:	2.46 %	15.28 g	7.64 g

CALORIE BREAKDOWN			
Energy (calories):	Total = 569.00 kcal	Per one serving = 284.50 kcal	
Calorie breakdown:	Percentagewise	Total	Per 1 serving
Protein:	29 %	165.00 kcal	82.50 kcal
Fat:	61 %	346.00 kcal	173.00 kcal
Carbohydrates:	10 %	59.00 kcal	29.50 kcal

CARBOHYDRATES				
	Per cent of total carbohydrates mass	Per cent of total weight	Total	Per 1 serving
Total Carbohydrates:		2.46 %	15.28 g	7.64 g
Dietary Fiber:	32.72 %	0.81 %	5.00 g	2.50 g
Sugars(net carbs):	31.02 %	**0.76 %**	**4.74 g**	**2.37 g**

These recipes are some of the best keto breakfasts that you will surely enjoy. They are mostly easy, and best of all they are meat-free and also follow the ketogenic diet.

Here are some of the recipes for you to munch on during your snack time.

16. Apple Cinnamon Bars

This is a gluten-free, vegetarian dish which is also sugar-free.

Ingredients
- 1 cup of pecans
- 1/4 cup of dried apples, frozen
- 1 cup of water
- 1/4 cup of butter, softened
- 1 tsp of vanilla extract
- 1/2 tsp cinnamon
- 2 tbsp of erythritol
- 1 ½ tsp of baking powder
- 1 tbsp of ground flax seed

Instructions
- Preheat the oven to 350 °F.
- Grease a brownie pan well.
- Add all ingredients to a blender and process until smooth.
- Pour the blended mixture into the brownie pan and bake it for about 45 minutes.
- Let it cool and serve.

GENERAL			
Servings quantity: 12 (12 brownies)			
Weight:	Total = 458.00 g	Per one serving = 38.17 g	
Mass fraction:	Percentagewise	Total	Per 1 serving
Protein:	2.42 %	11.10 g	0.93 g
Fat:	26.29 %	120.39 g	10.03 g
Carbohydrates:	12.89 %	59.04 g	4.92 g

CALORIE BREAKDOWN			
Energy (calories):	Total = 1204.00 kcal	Per one serving = 100.33 kcal	
Calorie breakdown:	Percentagewise	Total	Per 1 serving
Protein:	3 %	39.00 kcal	3.25 kcal
Fat:	85 %	1027.00 kcal	85.58 kcal
Carbohydrates:	11 %	127.00 kcal	10.58 kcal

CARBOHYDRATES				
	Per cent of total carbohydrates mass	Per cent of total weight	Total	Per 1 serving
Total Carbohydrates:		12.89 %	59.04 g	4.92 g
Dietary Fiber:	23.88 %	3.08 %	14.10 g	1.18 g
Sugars(net carbs):	28.68 %	3.70 %	16.93 g	1.41 g

17. Linzer Cookies

Cookies make for a great munching snack, and this low-carb, vegetarian option is healthy too!

Ingredients

For the cookies

- 3 ounces of buttery spread, soft
- 2 tbsp of erythritol
- 1 tbsp almond extract
- 6 tbsp coconut flour
- 2 tbsp of cream cheese, soft

For the filling

- ¼ cup of sugar-free raspberry jam

Instructions

- Preheat the oven to 350 °F.
- Mix together the butter, cream cheese, almond extract, and sweetener.
- Now, thoroughly mix in the coconut flour. Knead it for some time
- Now roll out the dough until it is about 5 mm thick.
- Now, using a cookie cutter, cut 10 "bottom" pieces and 10 "top" pieces.
- Place on cookie sheet, and bake for about 10 minutes.
- Remove from the oven and let cool for about 30 minutes.
- Spread 1 tsp of the jam on a "bottom" cookie, and then top with a "top" cookie. Repeat until all cookies are used.
- Serve.

GENERAL			
Servings quantity: 10 (10 cookies)			
Weight:	Total = 261.00 g	Per one serving = 26.10 g	
Mass fraction:	Percentagewise	Total	Per 1 serving
Protein:	3.16 %	8.25 g	0.83 g
Fat:	26.66 %	69.58 g	6.96 g
Carbohydrates:	26.50 %	69.17 g	6.92 g

CALORIE BREAKDOWN			
Energy (calories):	Total = 850.00 kcal	Per one serving = 85.00 kcal	
Calorie breakdown:	Percentagewise	Total	Per 1 serving
Protein:	4 %	34.20 kcal	3.42 kcal
Fat:	74 %	627.80 kcal	62.78 kcal
Carbohydrates:	12 %	104.00 kcal	10.40 kcal

CARBOHYDRATES				
	Per cent of total carbohydrates mass	Per cent of total weight	Total	Per 1 serving
Total Carbohydrates:		26.50 %	69.17 g	6.92 g
Dietary Fiber:	39.03 %	10.34 %	27.00 g	2.70 g
Sugars(net carbs):	5.86 %	**1.55 %**	**4.05 g**	**0.41 g**

18. Chocolate Protein Balls

Did you just hear chocolate? Yes, we bet you did!

Ingredients

- 90 g (2 scoops) of chocolate protein
- 1 cup of creamed coconut
- 1/2 tsp of mint extract
- ¼ cup of ground flax seed
- 2 tbsp of cocoa powder
- ½ tsp of vanilla extract

Instructions

- Add the creamed coconut to a large mixing bowl.
- Now, add the mint extract and the vanilla extract, and mix well.
- Add the flax seeds and the chocolate protein and knead the dough thoroughly.
- Make approximately 24 balls from this dough and keep them refrigerated for about 15 minutes.
- Roll the balls in cocoa powder.
- Serve.

GENERAL			
Servings quantity: 24 (24 protein balls)			
Weight:	Total = 373.50 g	Per one serving = 15.56 g	
Mass fraction:	Percentagewise	Total	Per 1 serving
Protein:	24.03 %	89.74 g	3.74 g
Fat:	51.28 %	191.54 g	7.98 g
Carbohydrates:	17.90 %	66.86 g	2.79 g

CALORIE BREAKDOWN			
Energy (calories):	Total = 2278.00 kcal	Per one serving = 94.92 kcal	
Calorie breakdown:	Percentagewise	Total	Per 1 serving
Protein:	22 %	490.74 kcal	20.45 kcal
Fat:	71 %	1610.21 kcal	67.09 kcal
Carbohydrates:	8 %	171.06 kcal	7.13 kcal

CARBOHYDRATES				
	Per cent of total carbohydrates mass	Per cent of total weight	Total	Per 1 serving
Total Carbohydrates:		17.90 %	66.86 g	2.79 g
Dietary Fiber:	53.32 %	9.54 %	35.65 g	1.49 g
Sugars(net carbs):	33.48 %	**5.99 %**	**22.39 g**	**0.93 g**

19. Heirloom Tomato Tart

Here is another vegetarian recipe which makes for a scrumptious snack.

Ingredients

For the crust
- 2 eggs
- ¾ cup of coconut flour
- ½ cup of coconut oil
- ½ tsp of salt

For the filling
- 4 ounces of tomatoes, heirloom
- 3 ounces of cheese
- Salt and pepper to taste

Instructions
- Preheat the oven to 350 °F.
- Mix all of the ingredients for the crust together.
- Press the mixture into a pan and evenly spread out, and let it bake for 20 minutes.
- Remove the crust from the oven, and sprinkle cheese on top.
- Cut the tomatoes into ¼" slices, and then place them on the top of the cheese.
- Add salt and pepper along with any other spices you like, such as oregano, for example.
- Cover pan and bake for 20 minutes.
- Let it cool.
- Serve.

GENERAL			
Servings quantity: 2			
Weight:	Total = 489.00 g	Per one serving = 244.50 g	
Mass fraction:	Percentagewise	Total	Per 1 serving
Protein:	9.29 %	45.45 g	22.73 g
Fat:	32.43 %	158.56 g	79.28 g
Carbohydrates:	11.70 %	57.21 g	28.61 g

CALORIE BREAKDOWN			
Energy (calories):	Total = 1804.00 kcal	Per one serving = 902.00 kcal	
Calorie breakdown:	Percentagewise	Total	Per 1 serving
Protein:	10 %	184.40 kcal	92.20 kcal
Fat:	77 %	1389.60 kcal	694.80 kcal
Carbohydrates:	13 %	230.00 kcal	115.00 kcal

CARBOHYDRATES				
	Per cent of total carbohydrates mass	Per cent of total weight	Total	Per 1 serving
Total Carbohydrates:		11.70 %	57.21 g	28.61 g
Dietary Fiber:	56.81 %	6.65 %	32.50 g	16.25 g
Sugars(net carbs):	11.54 %	1.35 %	6.60 g	3.30 g

20. Kale Chips

These kale chips are nut-free and even yeast-free and are delectable to taste.
A dehydrator needed for this recipe.

Ingredients
- 8 cups of kale, chopped but raw
- ¼ cup of raw parsley, roughly chopped
- 3 cloves of garlic
- ½ cup of raw hemp seeds, hulled
- ½ cup of raw sesame seeds, hulled
- 2 tbsp lemon juice
- 2 tsp spirulina
- ½ tsp salt
- ¼ cup of water

Instructions
- Add water, hemp seeds, and lemon juice to a blender. Blend well until you get a smooth mixture.
- Now, add parsley, spirulina, salt, and garlic and blend again.
- Pour in sesame seeds and blend some more.
- Place chopped kale in a bowl. Now, scoop the blended mixture prepared above into the bowl until the kale is completely coated.
- In a single layer, place the coated kale in a dehydrator until it is completely done. It can take about 8 hours or so.
- Serve.

GENERAL			
Servings quantity: 4			
Weight (after dehydration):	Total = 367.00 g	Per one serving = 91.75 g	
Mass fraction:	Percentagewise	Total	Per 1 serving
Protein:	18.01 %	66.10 g	16.53 g
Fat:	22.75 %	83.49 g	20.87 g
Carbohydrates:	19.31 %	70.85 g	17.71 g

CALORIE BREAKDOWN			
Energy (calories):	Total = 1055.00 kcal	Per one serving = 263.75 kcal	
Calorie breakdown:	Percentagewise	Total	Per 1 serving
Protein:	23 %	239.00 kcal	59.75 kcal
Fat:	56 %	591.00 kcal	147.75 kcal
Carbohydrates:	22 %	228.00 kcal	57.00 kcal

CARBOHYDRATES				
	Per cent of total carbohydrates mass	Per cent of total weight	Total	Per 1 serving
Total Carbohydrates:		19.31 %	70.85 g	17.71 g
Dietary Fiber:	52.08 %	10.05 %	36.90 g	9.23 g
Sugars(net carbs):	19.21 %	3.71 %	13.61 g	3.40 g

21. Green Bean Fries

If you're really health-conscious and looking for a snack you won't have to fuss over, look no further.

Ingredients
- 1 large egg
- 12 oz of green beans
- ½ tsp of garlic powder
- ⅔ cup of grated parmesan
- ¼ tsp of paprika
- ¼ tsp black pepper
- ½ tsp salt

Instructions
- Preheat oven to 400 °F.
- Rinse the green beans, pat dry, and snip the ends.
- In a shallow bowl or on a plate, mix the grated parmesan cheese and seasonings evenly.
- Whisk egg in a large bowl.
- Dredge the green beans thoroughly in the egg, letting excess egg drip off.
- Press the green beans into the cheese mixture.
- Sprinkle extra cheese on green beans manually if necessary.
- Place the beans on a greased baking sheet.
- Bake for 10 minutes until cheese is slightly golden in color.
- Serve.

GENERAL			
Servings quantity: 2			
Weight:	Total = 463.00 g	Per one serving = 231.50 g	
Mass fraction:	Percentagewise	Total	Per 1 serving
Protein:	6.90 %	31.96 g	15.98 g
Fat:	5.24 %	24.26 g	12.13 g
Carbohydrates:	7.62 %	35.26 g	17.63 g

CALORIE BREAKDOWN			
Energy (calories):	Total = 467.00 kcal	Per one serving = 233.50 kcal	
Calorie breakdown:	Percentagewise	Total	Per 1 serving
Protein:	27 %	125.00 kcal	62.50 kcal
Fat:	46 %	214.00 kcal	107.00 kcal
Carbohydrates:	28 %	129.00 kcal	64.50 kcal

CARBOHYDRATES				
	Per cent of total carbohydrates mass	Per cent of total weight	Total	Per 1 serving
Total Carbohydrates:		7.62 %	35.26 g	17.63 g
Dietary Fiber:	27.51 %	2.10 %	9.70 g	4.85 g
Sugars(net carbs):	32.42 %	2.47 %	11.43 g	5.72 g

22. Salted Almond and Coconut Bark

If you like sweet and savory, this one is worth the extra effort.

Ingredients

- ½ cup of coconut butter
- 3.5 ounces of dark chocolate
- ½ cup of almonds
- ½ tsp of almond extract
- ½ cup of unsweetened flaked coconut
- 10 drops of liquid stevia
- Sea salt to taste

Instructions

- Preheat the oven to 350°F.
- Line a baking sheet with foil. Spread the coconut and almonds on it.
- Toast in the oven for 5 to 8 minutes.
- Stir occasionally to prevent burning.
- After they're thoroughly toasted, set aside to cool.
- Melt the dark chocolate in a double boiler.
- Stir in the coconut butter.
- Add almond extract and liquid stevia. Mix well and set aside.
- Line a baking sheet with parchment paper and pour the chocolate mixture on top.
- Spread evenly using the back of a spoon or spatula.
- Sprinkle the roasted almonds and coconut flakes evenly on top and gently press them in.
- Sprinkle with sea salt. Refrigerate for 1 hour.

GENERAL		
Servings quantity: 6 (each serving is about 1 $2/3$ ounces)		
Weight:	Total = 281.76 g	Per one serving = 46.96 g
Mass fraction:	Percentagewise	Total	Per 1 serving
Protein:	6.56 %	18.49 g	3.08 g
Fat:	50.04 %	140.99 g	23.50 g
Carbohydrates:	29.92 %	84.30 g	14.05 g

CALORIE BREAKDOWN		
Energy (calories):	Total = 1641.86 kcal	Per one serving = 273.64 kcal
Calorie breakdown:	Percentagewise	Total	Per 1 serving
Protein:	6 %	105.63 kcal	17.60 kcal
Fat:	65 %	1074.18 kcal	179.03 kcal
Carbohydrates:	28 %	454.55 kcal	75.76 kcal

CARBOHYDRATES				
	Per cent of total carbohydrates mass	Per cent of total weight	Total	Per 1 serving
Total Carbohydrates:		29.92 %	84.30 g	14.05 g
Dietary Fiber:	43.01 %	12.87 %	36.26 g	6.04 g
Sugars(net carbs):	40.88 %	**12.23 %**	**34.46 g**	**5.74 g**

23. Easy Guacamole

A summertime staple, this one is quick and zesty.

Ingredients
- 2 avocados
- 6 grape tomatoes
- ¼ cup of diced red onion
- 1 juiced lime
- 1 garlic clove
- 1 tbsp of olive oil
- 5 sprigs of fresh cilantro
- ¼ tsp of salt
- ⅛ tsp of crushed red pepper
- ⅛ tsp of black pepper

Instructions
- Peel and pit the avocados.
- Mash the avocados in a mixing bowl.
- Dice the grape tomatoes and red onions evenly.
- Add the diced tomatoes and onions to the mashed avocados.
- Add the olive oil.
- Using a garlic press, mince the garlic clove and add to the mixture.
- Mix well.
- Add the lime juice and cilantro and mix again.
- Finally, season with salt, pepper, and crushed red pepper.

GENERAL			
Servings quantity: 2			
Weight:	Total = 555.00 g	Per one serving = 277.50 g	
Mass fraction:	Percentagewise	Total	Per 1 serving
Protein:	1.71 %	9.47 g	4.74 g
Fat:	13.10 %	72.71 g	36.36 g
Carbohydrates:	7.99 %	44.37 g	22.19 g

CALORIE BREAKDOWN			
Energy (calories):	Total = 803.00 kcal	Per one serving = 401.50 kcal	
Calorie breakdown:	Percentagewise	Total	Per 1 serving
Protein:	4 %	31.00 kcal	15.50 kcal
Fat:	77 %	615.00 kcal	307.50 kcal
Carbohydrates:	20 %	157.00 kcal	78.50 kcal

CARBOHYDRATES				
	Per cent of total carbohydrates mass	Per cent of total weight	Total	Per 1 serving
Total Carbohydrates:		7.99 %	44.37 g	22.19 g
Dietary Fiber:	64.68 %	5.17 %	28.70 g	14.35 g
Sugars(net carbs):	13.77 %	1.10 %	6.11 g	3.06 g

24. Coconut Butter Cups

Seriously decadent sweet goodness.

Ingredients

- tbsp + 4 tsp of coconut oil
- 2 tbsp of erythritol
- tbsp of cocoa powder
- 2 tbsp of coconut butter
- 1 pinch of salt

Instructions

- Mix 4 tbsp coconut oil, the erythritol, and the cocoa powder in a bowl until smooth.
- Add salt and stir to evenly distribute.
- Coat 4 cups of a silicone cupcake mold with coconut butter (1/2 tbsp per cup).
- Pour 2/3 of the cocoa mixture into the cupcake molds, dividing evenly among the four cups. Be sure to tilt and turn the mold until each cup is entirely coated.
- Freeze for 5 minutes.
- When the bottom layer has hardened completely, pour a tsp of coconut oil in each mold.
- Place it in the freezer for a few more minutes.
- Take the leftover cocoa mixture and cover the solidified coconut oil.
- Freeze again for 5 minutes.
- Pop from molds to serve.

GENERAL			
Servings quantity: 4 coconut butter cups			
Weight:	Total = 155.00 g	Per one serving = 38.75 g	
Mass fraction:	Percentagewise	Total	Per 1 serving
Protein:	4.02 %	6.23 g	1.56 g
Fat:	60.23 %	93.36 g	23.34 g
Carbohydrates:	28.07 %	43.51 g	10.88 g

CALORIE BREAKDOWN			
Energy (calories):	Total = 859.00 kcal	Per one serving = 214.75 kcal	
Calorie breakdown:	Percentagewise	Total	Per 1 serving
Protein:	3 %	21.78 kcal	5.44 kcal
Fat:	90 %	773.00 kcal	193.25 kcal
Carbohydrates:	8 %	65.22 kcal	16.31 kcal

CARBOHYDRATES				
	Per cent of total carbohydrates mass	Per cent of total weight	Total	Per 1 serving
Total Carbohydrates:		28.07 %	43.51 g	10.88 g
Dietary Fiber:	29.88 %	8.39 %	13.00 g	3.25 g
Sugars(net carbs):	5.47 %	1.54 %	2.38 g	0.60 g

25. Keto Protein Shake

Shakes are always good for a quick snack.

Ingredients

- 1 tbsp of cocoa powder
- 1 scoop of chocolate protein powder
- 1 cup of almond milk
- 1 tbsp of peanut butter
- 2 tsp of erythritol
- ice cubes
- 1 tbsp of coconut oil

Instructions

- Mix the cocoa powder and the chocolate protein powder in a large bowl.
- In a blender, add the almond milk, peanut butter, erythritol, and coconut oil, and mix briefly.
- Transfer the mixed powders into the blender and mix.
- Add ice cubes and blend thoroughly.

Note: You can choose any main liquid for your shake – water, cream, coconut milk, almond milk, or milk. We recommend sticking with lower carb options.

GENERAL			
Servings quantity: 1			
Weight:	Total = 379.00 g	Per one serving = 379.00 g	
Mass fraction:	Percentagewise	Total	Per 1 serving
Protein:	8.44 %	31.97 g	31.97 g
Fat:	7.13 %	27.01 g	27.01 g
Carbohydrates:	6.03 %	22.85 g	22.85 g

CALORIE BREAKDOWN			
Energy (calories):	Total = 412.00 kcal	Per one serving = 412.00 kcal	
Calorie breakdown:	Percentagewise	Total	Per 1 serving
Protein:	32 %	133.08 kcal	133.08 kcal
Fat:	55 %	226.42 kcal	226.42 kcal
Carbohydrates:	13 %	52.50 kcal	52.50 kcal

CARBOHYDRATES				
	Per cent of total carbohydrates mass	Per cent of total weight	Total	Per 1 serving
Total Carbohydrates:		6.03 %	22.85 g	22.85 g
Dietary Fiber:	13.13 %	0.79 %	3.00 g	3.00 g
Sugars(net carbs):	28.84 %	**1.74 %**	**6.59 g**	**6.59 g**

26. Sugar-Free Peanut Butter Fudge

We know that merely mentioning dessert might elicit serious food cravings, but this recipe is completely sugar-free and adheres to ketogenic recommendations as well.

Ingredients

- ¼ cup of unsweetened vanilla almond milk
- 1 cup of unsweetened peanut butter
- 1 cup of coconut oil

Instructions

- In a microwave-safe bowl, combine peanut butter and coconut oil. Heat gently to soften.
- Once heated, transfer to a blender.
- Add the almond milk and blend thoroughly.
- Pour the mix into a parchment-lined pan.
- Refrigerate for 2 hours.
- Cut into 12 pieces and serve.

GENERAL			
Servings quantity: 12 (each serving is about 1½ ounces)			
Weight:	Total = 534.00 g	Per one serving = 44.50 g	
Mass fraction:	Percentagewise	Total	Per 1 serving
Protein:	11.78 %	62.89 g	5.24 g
Fat:	66.93 %	357.43 g	29.79 g
Carbohydrates:	8.15 %	43.52 g	3.63 g

CALORIE BREAKDOWN			
Energy (calories):	Total = 3444.75 kcal	Per one serving = 287.06 kcal	
Calorie breakdown:	Percentagewise	Total	Per 1 serving
Protein:	6 %	219.19 kcal	18.27 kcal
Fat:	88 %	3046.56 kcal	253.88 kcal
Carbohydrates:	5 %	177.00 kcal	14.75 kcal

CARBOHYDRATES				
	Per cent of total carbohydrates mass	Per cent of total weight	Total	Per 1 serving
Total Carbohydrates:		8.15 %	43.52 g	3.63 g
Dietary Fiber:	35.85 %	2.92 %	15.60 g	1.30 g
Sugars(net carbs):	18.29 %	**1.49 %**	**7.96 g**	**0.66 g**

27. Pecan Fat Baby-Bombs

This can be taken for lunch or also as a snack depending on your appetite.

Ingredients

- 4 toasted pecan halves
- 1 pinch of sea salt
- ½ tbsp of unsalted grass-fed butter

Instructions

- Spread approximately half of the grass-fed butter between two pecan halves and press together.
- Now sprinkle a bit of sea salt over the pecan "sandwich." Repeat with remaining two pecan halves.
- Serve. Thanks to these two baby-bombs you won't be hungry for a few hours.

GENERAL			
Servings quantity: 1			
Weight:	Total = 16.00 g	Per one serving = 16.00 g	
Mass fraction:	Percentagewise	Total	Per 1 serving
Protein:	3.94 %	0.63 g	0.63 g
Fat:	63.88 %	10.22 g	10.22 g
Carbohydrates:	5.13 %	0.82 g	0.82 g

CALORIE BREAKDOWN			
Energy (calories):	Total = 94.00 kcal	Per one serving = 94.00 kcal	
Calorie breakdown:	Percentagewise	Total	Per 1 serving
Protein:	2 %	2.00 kcal	2.00 kcal
Fat:	94 %	88.00 kcal	88.00 kcal
Carbohydrates:	3 %	3.00 kcal	3.00 kcal

CARBOHYDRATES				
	Per cent of total carbohydrates mass	Per cent of total weight	Total	Per 1 serving
Total Carbohydrates:		5.13 %	0.82 g	0.82 g
Dietary Fiber:	73.17 %	3.75 %	0.60 g	0.60 g
Sugars(net carbs):	**30.49 %**	**1.56 %**	**0.25 g**	**0.25 g**

Vegetarian Keto Lunch Recipes

Now that we are done with breakfast and snacks, it is about time that we shift our focus to lunch recipes.

28. Jackfruit and Cauliflower Taco Bowls

This recipe is simple and easy to make and the taste is quite delectable too.

Ingredients

- 1 package(12 oz) of cauliflower rice
- 1 can of young jackfruit in water (drained WT = 9.8 oz)
- 1 cup of frozen kale
- 1 tbsp of taco seasoning
- 1 tbsp olive oil
- Garlic and onion powder to taste
- (optional) Cheese and guacamole for serving

Instructions

- Drain the water from the can of jackfruit. Chop the jackfruit into small pieces.
- Add all the ingredients except the vegan cheese and guacamole to a sauté pan. Sauté it until the cauliflower has turned tender.
- Serve it with guacamole and/or vegan cheese if desired.

GENERAL		
Servings quantity: 4		
Weight:	Total = 768.00 g	Per one serving = 192.00 g
Mass fraction:	Percentagewise	Total	Per 1 serving
Protein:	2.06 %	15.79 g	3.95 g
Fat:	1.84 %	14.11 g	3.53 g
Carbohydrates:	7.47 %	57.34 g	14.34 g

CALORIE BREAKDOWN		
Energy (calories):	Total = 407.00 kcal	Per one serving = 101.75 kcal
Calorie breakdown:	Percentagewise	Total	Per 1 serving
Protein:	51 %	209.00 kcal	52.25 kcal
Fat:	30 %	124.00 kcal	31.00 kcal
Carbohydrates:	18 %	74.00 kcal	18.50 kcal

CARBOHYDRATES				
	Per cent of total carbohydrates mass	Per cent of total weight	Total	Per 1 serving
Total Carbohydrates:		7.47 %	57.34 g	14.34 g
Dietary Fiber:	68.54 %	5.12 %	39.30 g	9.83 g
Sugars(net carbs):	**14.93 %**	**1.11 %**	**8.56 g**	**2.14 g**

29. Bell Pepper Basil Pizza

Who doesn't love pizza? This perfect recipe lets you satisfy your taste buds while still sticking to the diet.

Ingredients

The pizza base

- ½ cup of almond flour
- 1 large egg
- 2 tbsp of parmesan cheese, fresh
- 6 ounces of mozzarella cheese
- 2 tbsp of cream cheese
- 2 tbsp of psyllium husk
- 1 tsp of Italian seasoning
- ½ tsp salt
- ½ tsp pepper

For the toppings

- 2/3 bell pepper, medium
- ¼ cup of marinara sauce
- 4 ounces of cheddar cheese, shredded
- 3 tbsp of chopped basil, fresh
- 1 medium vine tomato

Instructions
- Preheat the oven to 400 °F.
- Microwave the mozzarella cheese for about 45 seconds.
- Now, add all the pizza base ingredients to the melted cheese and mix well.
- Roll out the dough in the shape of a circle.
- Bake it for 10 minutes and then remove from the oven.
- Now, add the toppings and bake it for an additional 10 minutes.
- Remove the pizza from the oven and let it cool.

GENERAL			
Servings quantity: 2			
Weight:	Total = 701.00 g	Per one serving = 350.50 g	
Mass fraction:	Percentagewise	Total	Per 1 serving
Protein:	12.79 %	89.66 g	44.83 g
Fat:	16.91 %	118.52 g	59.26 g
Carbohydrates:	6.77 %	47.48 g	23.74 g

CALORIE BREAKDOWN			
Energy (calories):	Total = 1586.00 kcal	Per one serving = 793.00 kcal	
Calorie breakdown:	Percentagewise	Total	Per 1 serving
Protein:	23 %	363.00 kcal	181.50 kcal
Fat:	66 %	1041.00 kcal	520.50 kcal
Carbohydrates:	11 %	181.00 kcal	90.50 kcal

CARBOHYDRATES

	Per cent of total carbohydrates mass	Per cent of total weight	Total	Per 1 serving
Total Carbohydrates:		6.77 %	47.48 g	23.74 g
Dietary Fiber:	49.07 %	3.32 %	23.30 g	11.65 g
Sugars(net carbs):	21.95 %	**1.49 %**	**10.42 g**	**5.21 g**

30. Collard Wraps

If you love collard, this is a great way to satiate your appetite for lunch.

Ingredients

For the tzatziki sauce

- 1 cup of full-fat plain Greek yogurt
- ¼ whole, grated and seeded cucumber
- 2 tbsp olive oil
- 1 tsp garlic powder
- 2 tbsp of minced fresh dill
- 1 tbsp of white vinegar

For the wrap

- ½ cup of diced red onions
- 4 cherry tomatoes, halved
- 4 washed large collard green leaves
- ½ block feta that has been cut into 1 inch thick strips
- 1 medium cucumber, julienned
- 8 kalamata olives, halved
- ½ medium red bell pepper, julienned

Instructions

- Remove the water from the cucumber completely after it has been grated. You can do this by pressing the grated cucumber with paper towels until you they are relatively dry.
- Mix together all ingredients required for the tzatziki sauce and store in the fridge.
- Now, wash the collard leaves and then remove the stem from the leaves.
- Place 2 tbsp of tzatziki sauce on the center of the collard leaf wrap, and then spread it out evenly.
- Now, add peppers, cucumber, feta, olives, onion, and tomatoes in the center of the wrap.
- Now, fold like you would a burrito.
- Slice it in half and serve it with any additional tzatziki sauce.

GENERAL			
Servings quantity: 4			
Weight:	Total = 1040.00 g	Per one serving = 260.00 g	
Mass fraction:	Percentagewise	Total	Per 1 serving
Protein:	3.33 %	34.67 g	8.67 g
Fat:	6.19 %	64.41 g	16.10 g
Carbohydrates:	4.81 %	50.00 g	12.50 g

CALORIE BREAKDOWN			
Energy (calories):	Total = 889.00 kcal	Per one serving = 222.25 kcal	
Calorie breakdown:	Percentagewise	Total	Per 1 serving
Protein:	15 %	134.00 kcal	33.50 kcal
Fat:	64 %	566.00 kcal	141.50 kcal
Carbohydrates:	21 %	188.00 kcal	47.00 kcal

CARBOHYDRATES				
	Per cent of total carbohydrates mass	Per cent of total weight	Total	Per 1 serving
Total Carbohydrates:		4.81 %	50.00 g	12.50 g
Dietary Fiber:	26.00 %	1.25 %	13.00 g	3.25 g
Sugars(net carbs):	**56.28 %**	**2.71 %**	**28.14 g**	**7.04 g**

31. Roasted Cauliflower with Burrata

If you have a thing for cauliflowers, you are going to love this dish immensely!

Ingredients

- 1 large head (about 2 pounds) of cauliflower, washed, cored, and sliced
- 2 tbsp of fresh thyme
- 1 tsp of sea salt
- 1 tsp ground pepper
- 2 tbsp of melted coconut oil

Instructions

- Preheat the oven to 425 °F.
- Add the cauliflower slices to a bowl.
- Now slowly drizzle the oil over the cauliflower and then sprinkle with thyme leaves, salt, and pepper.
- Toss to coat.
- Layer the coated cauliflower slices evenly on a baking sheet.
- Roast in the oven until the cauliflower has caramelized.
- Garnish with thyme leaves and serve.

GENERAL			
Servings quantity: 4			
Weight:	Total = 948.00 g	Per one serving = 237.00 g	
Mass fraction:	Percentagewise	Total	Per 1 serving
Protein:	1.89 %	17.92 g	4.48 g
Fat:	3.15 %	29.90 g	7.48 g
Carbohydrates:	5.03 %	47.73 g	11.93 g

CALORIE BREAKDOWN			
Energy (calories):	Total = 472.00 kcal	Per one serving = 118.00 kcal	
Calorie breakdown:	Percentagewise	Total	Per 1 serving
Protein:	9 %	44.00 kcal	11.00 kcal
Fat:	54 %	257.00 kcal	64.25 kcal
Carbohydrates:	36 %	169.00 kcal	42.25 kcal

CARBOHYDRATES				
	Per cent of total carbohydrates mass	Per cent of total weight	Total	Per 1 serving
Total Carbohydrates:		5.03 %	47.73 g	11.93 g
Dietary Fiber:	40.65 %	2.05 %	19.40 g	4.85 g
Sugars(net carbs):	36.33 %	1.83 %	17.34 g	4.34 g

32. Ketogenic Mac and Cheese

We all know how much each one of us loves Mac and cheese. This recipe here is grain-free and absolutely keto-friendly.

Ingredients

- ½ cup of onion, minced
- ½ cup heavy cream
- 1 lb of jicama(yam bean) cut into ¼" x ¼" x 1" pieces
- ½ cup crème fraiche
- 3 cups of shredded cheddar cheese
- 2 tbsp of yellow mustard
- ½ tsp black pepper
- ½ tsp of sea salt

Instructions

- Take a medium-sized bowl and add crème fraiche to it. Now, add salt, heavy cream, black pepper, and yellow mustard.
- Mix well until combined.
- Now, add in onion and jicama and mix until they're coated well.
- Finally, add the shredded cheese and mix well to blend uniformly.
- Pour into a baking pan that has been well greased and bake it at 350 °F for about 45 minutes.
- Serve.

GENERAL			
Servings quantity: 4			
Weight:	Total = 1038.00 g	Per one serving = 259.50 g	
Mass fraction:	Percentagewise	Total	Per 1 serving
Protein:	8.73 %	90.57 g	22.64 g
Fat:	15.52 %	161.12 g	40.28 g
Carbohydrates:	5.76 %	59.75 g	14.94 g

CALORIE BREAKDOWN			
Energy (calories):	Total = 2032.00 kcal	Per one serving = 508.00 kcal	
Calorie breakdown:	Percentagewise	Total	Per 1 serving
Protein:	18 %	357.00 kcal	89.25 kcal
Fat:	71 %	1440.00 kcal	360.00 kcal
Carbohydrates:	12 %	236.00 kcal	59.00 kcal

CARBOHYDRATES				
	Per cent of total carbohydrates mass	Per cent of total weight	Total	Per 1 serving
Total Carbohydrates:		5.76 %	59.75 g	14.94 g
Dietary Fiber:	42.18 %	2.43 %	25.20 g	6.30 g
Sugars(net carbs):	29.77 %	1.71 %	17.79 g	4.45 g

33. Zucchini Rolls

An easy to make recipe, this one is ideal for your lunchtime.

Ingredients

- ½ cup of drained sun-dried tomatoes
- 3 organic baby zucchini
- ½ cup of fresh basil
- 4 tbsp of raspberry vinegar
- 1 cup of soft goat cheese

Instructions

- Preheat the oven to 400 °F.
- Then, slice the zucchini lengthwise into long, thin, even strips, so that they can be used to roll up.
- Place in a bowl and then add vinegar, ensuring that the zucchini strips are covered on all sides. Leave it to rest for 10 minutes.
- Remove zucchini from bowl, and lay on a flat surface or plate. Top each zucchini strip with goat cheese, sun-dried tomatoes, and basil.
- Carefully wrap the zucchini rolls and insert a toothpick and serve.

GENERAL			
Servings quantity: 2			
Weight:	Total = 378.00 g	Per one serving = 189.00 g	
Mass fraction:	Percentagewise	Total	Per 1 serving
Protein:	13.40 %	50.64 g	25.32 g
Fat:	13.99 %	52.87 g	26.44 g
Carbohydrates:	5.93 %	22.40 g	11.20 g

CALORIE BREAKDOWN			
Energy (calories):	Total = 729.00 kcal	Per one serving = 364.50 kcal	
Calorie breakdown:	Percentagewise	Total	Per 1 serving
Protein:	28 %	207.00 kcal	103.50 kcal
Fat:	64 %	464.00 kcal	232.00 kcal
Carbohydrates:	8 %	59.00 kcal	29.50 kcal

CARBOHYDRATES				
	Per cent of total carbohydrates mass	Per cent of total weight	Total	Per 1 serving
Total Carbohydrates:		5.93 %	22.40 g	11.20 g
Dietary Fiber:	73.21 %	4.34 %	16.40 g	8.20 g
Sugars(net carbs):	63.35 %	3.75 %	14.19 g	7.10 g

34. Cream of Mushroom Soup

Soup can always be a great lunch as it is a filling and scrumptious choice.

Ingredients

- 1 ½ cups of white mushrooms, diced
- 2 cups of cauliflower florets
- ½ yellow onion, diced
- 1 2/3 cup of almond milk, unsweetened
- ½ tsp of extra virgin olive oil
- 1 tsp of onion powder
- ¼ tsp of rock salt
- Ground pepper

Instructions

- In a small saucepan, add milk, cauliflower, onion powder along with salt and pepper.
- Cover and cook over medium heat until it begins to boil.
- Now turn the heat to low and let it simmer for around 8 minutes.
- Add the contents to a food processor and make a puree.
- Now in another medium-sized saucepan, add mushrooms, oil, and onion. Heat it for about 8 minutes.
- Now, add pureed cauliflower mixture to this medium saucepan. Boil it for about 10 minutes.
- Serve.

GENERAL			
Servings quantity: 4			
Weight:	Total = 737.80 g	Per one serving = 184.45 g	
Mass fraction:	Percentagewise	Total	Per 1 serving
Protein:	1.33 %	9.83 g	2.46 g
Fat:	1.05 %	7.77 g	1.94 g
Carbohydrates:	2.55 %	18.84 g	4.71 g

CALORIE BREAKDOWN			
Energy (calories):	Total = 173.45 kcal	Per one serving = 43.36 kcal	
Calorie breakdown:	Percentagewise	Total	Per 1 serving
Protein:	22 %	38.95 kcal	9.74 kcal
Fat:	39 %	67.84 kcal	16.96 kcal
Carbohydrates:	38 %	66.67 kcal	16.67 kcal

CARBOHYDRATES				
	Per cent of total carbohydrates mass	Per cent of total weight	Total	Per 1 serving
Total Carbohydrates:		2.55 %	18.84 g	4.71 g
Dietary Fiber:	34.50 %	0.88 %	6.50 g	1.63 g
Sugars(net carbs):	45.49 %	1.16 %	8.57 g	2.14 g

35. Keto Noodles with Avocado Pesto

f you have a thing for pesto, this recipe can offer you a fulfilling lunch.

Ingredients for the avocado pesto

- ½ cup of fresh baby spinach leaves
- 1 half avocado
- 1 cloves of garlic
- ¼ cup of extra virgin olive oil
- 1/8 cup of fresh basil
- ½ tsp of salt

Instructions

- Add all of the pesto ingredients to a blender, and blend well. Adding the olive oil slowly, while the processor is running, will help keep the oil from separating and help it emulsify.
- Thus you've got about 1 cup of pesto sauce. You need ¼ cup of pesto per each bag of noodles.

Here are the nutrient facts of pesto:

GENERAL			
Servings quantity: 4 (one serving = 1/4 cup of pesto)			
Weight:	Total = 179.00 g	Per one serving = 44.75 g	
Mass fraction:	Percentagewise	Total	Per 1 serving
Protein:	1.27 %	2.27 g	0.57 g
Fat:	38.45 %	68.83 g	17.21 g
Carbohydrates:	5.69 %	10.19 g	2.55 g

CALORIE BREAKDOWN			
Energy (calories):	Total = 647.00 kcal	Per one serving = 161.75 kcal	
Calorie breakdown:	Percentagewise	Total	Per 1 serving
Protein:	1 %	9.00 kcal	2.25 kcal
Fat:	93 %	601.00 kcal	150.25 kcal
Carbohydrates:	6 %	37.00 kcal	9.25 kcal

CARBOHYDRATES				
	Per cent of total carbohydrates mass	Per cent of total weight	Total	Per 1 serving
Total Carbohydrates:		5.69 %	10.19 g	2.55 g
Dietary Fiber:	70.66 %	4.02 %	7.20 g	1.80 g
Sugars(net carbs):	7.56 %	**0.43 %**	**0.77 g**	**0.19 g**

Ingredients for the keto noodles

- one 16-ounce pack of kelp noodles
- ¼ cup of pesto

Instructions

- Take the kelp noodles and rinse it well. Soak them in water for about half an hour.

- When the noodles are done soaking, drain them. Add ¼ cup of pesto for every bag o noodles used.
- Mix both the noodles and pesto thoroughly.
- Serve.

Here are the nutrient facts of keto noodles with avocado pesto:

GENERAL			
Servings quantity: 4			
Weight:	Total = 498.75 g	Per one serving = 124.69 g	
Mass fraction:	Percentagewise	Total	Per 1 serving
Protein:	0.11 %	0.57 g	0.14 g
Fat:	3.45 %	17.21 g	4.30 g
Carbohydrates:	1.31 %	6.55 g	1.64 g

CALORIE BREAKDOWN			
Energy (calories):	Total = 185.75 kcal	Per one serving = 46.44 kcal	
Calorie breakdown:	Percentagewise	Total	Per 1 serving
Protein:	1 %	2.25 kcal	0.56 kcal
Fat:	81 %	150.25 kcal	37.56 kcal
Carbohydrates:	18 %	33.25 kcal	8.31 kcal

CARBOHYDRATES				
	Per cent of total carbohydrates mass	Per cent of total weight	Total	Per 1 serving
Total Carbohydrates:		1.31 %	6.55 g	1.64 g
Dietary Fiber:	88.58 %	1.16 %	5.80 g	1.45 g
Sugars(net carbs):	2.94 %	**0.04 %**	**0.19 g**	**0.05 g**

36. Low-Carb Pizza

Yes, you read correctly. You can even have pizza while on a ketogenic diet. All the more reason to stick with it, right?

Ingredients

- 1 medium (about 20-21 ounces) head of cauliflower
- 1 cup of chia seeds
- 1 cup of water
- tbsp of olive oil
- 1 tsp of sea salt
- ½ cup of cream cheese
- 2 cloves of garlic, minced
- ½ cup of grated parmesan cheese
- ½ cup of heavy cream

Instructions

- Remove all the cauliflower florets from the stem.
- Using a food processor, chop them into smaller pieces.
- Grind the chia seeds into flour.
- Combine the chia flour, chopped cauliflower, water, olive oil, and salt in a mixing bowl.
- Mix well until you get a smooth dough.
- Let rest for 20 minutes.
- Coat a cookie sheet with olive oil.
- Roll the dough out until it's an even layer, and place on the cookie sheet.
- Bake at 200 °F for 30 to 40 minutes.
- The crust should be cooked thoroughly. If not, keep a close watch while baking it longer.
- When the crust is ready, remove from oven.
- Preheat oven to 400 °F.
- In a food processor, mix the parmesan, cream cheese, heavy cream, and garlic until a smooth paste is formed.
- Spread it on the pizza crust.
- Bake at 400 °F for 10 minutes.

Note: You can add keto-friendly vegetable toppings as desired.

GENERAL			
Servings quantity: 5			
Weight:	Total = 1176.00 g	Per one serving = 235.20 g	
Mass fraction:	Percentagewise	Total	Per 1 serving
Protein:	5.00 %	58.76 g	11.75 g
Fat:	14.20 %	166.95 g	33.39 g
Carbohydrates:	9.15 %	107.58 g	21.52 g

CALORIE BREAKDOWN		
Energy (calories):	Total = 2083.00 kcal	Per one serving = 416.60 kcal

Calorie breakdown:	Percentagewise	Total	Per 1 serving
Protein:	10 %	212.00 kcal	42.40 kcal
Fat:	70 %	1448.00 kcal	289.60 kcal
Carbohydrates:	20 %	422.00 kcal	84.40 kcal

CARBOHYDRATES				
	Per cent of total carbohydrates mass	Per cent of total weight	Total	Per 1 serving
Total Carbohydrates:		9.15 %	107.58 g	21.52 g
Dietary Fiber:	60.61 %	5.54 %	65.20 g	13.04 g
Sugars(net carbs):	13.98 %	**1.28 %**	**15.04 g**	**3.01 g**

37. Grilled Tomatoes with Apricot Jam

This can be used either as a snack or for lunch.

Ingredients

- 6 medium sized tomatoes (738g)
- 2 tsp of dried oregano (2g)
- 1 ½ oz of watercress for garnishing (43g)
- tsp of sugar-free apricot jam (18g)
- ½ oz of grated Gouda cheese (99g)
- 1 tbsp of olive oil (14g)
- salt and pepper to taste

Instructions

- Preheat oven to 350 °F.
- Cut the tomatoes into halves and place cut side up on a lightly greased baking tray.
- Spread jam on each of the tomato slices.
- Sprinkle the oregano and grated cheese on top.
- Bake for 25 minutes or until the cheese turns golden.
- Drizzle with olive oil and top with black pepper and salt.
- Garnish with watercress.

GENERAL			
Servings quantity: 4 (3 tomato halves per serving)			
Weight:	Total = 922.00 g	Per one serving = 230.50 g	
Mass fraction:	Percentagewise	Total	Per 1 serving
Protein:	3.57 %	32.91 g	8.23 g
Fat:	4.61 %	42.49 g	10.62 g
Carbohydrates:	4.45 %	41.03 g	10.26 g

CALORIE BREAKDOWN			
Energy (calories):	Total = 638.00 kcal	Per one serving = 159.50 kcal	
Calorie breakdown:	Percentagewise	Total	Per 1 serving
Protein:	20 %	125.00 kcal	31.25 kcal
Fat:	58 %	373.00 kcal	93.25 kcal
Carbohydrates:	21 %	137.00 kcal	34.25 kcal

CARBOHYDRATES				
	Per cent of total carbohydrates mass	Per cent of total weight	Total	Per 1 serving
Total Carbohydrates:		4.45 %	41.03 g	10.26 g
Dietary Fiber:	32.17 %	1.43 %	13.20 g	3.30 g
Sugars(net carbs):	53.16 %	**2.37 %**	**21.81 g**	**5.45 g**

38. Brie and Apple Crepes

This dish scores points for presentation too.

Ingredients

For the crepe batter
- oz of cream cheese
- ½ tsp of baking soda
- large eggs
- ¼ tsp of salt

For the toppings
- 2 oz of chopped pecans
- 1 small sweet apple, sliced
- 1 tbsp of unsalted butter
- oz of brie cheese, sliced
- ¼ tsp of cinnamon
- fresh mint leaves

Instructions

- Melt butter in a small pan.
- Toast the chopped pecans. Sprinkle cinnamon on top and mix
- Transfer pecans to a plate and let cool.
- Put all the batter ingredients in a blender and blend until smooth.
- Add a small amount of unsalted butter to a non-stick pan and heat on medium.
- Ladle some of the crepe batter into the pan. Swirl to spread evenly into a thin layer.
- Cook until the top seems to have dried, then flip it gently and cook the other side for few seconds. Transfer to a plate.
- Repeat the previous two steps until all of the batter is used.
- Arrange the apple slices and brie on one side of a crepe and top with roasted pecans. Fold crepe in half so toppings are sandwiched.
- Repeat for all the crepes.
- Garnish with mint.

GENERAL			
Servings quantity: 2			
Weight:	Total = 652.00 g	Per one serving = 326.00 g	
Mass fraction:	Percentagewise	Total	Per 1 serving
Protein:	9.38 %	61.14 g	30.57 g
Fat:	21.75 %	141.83 g	70.92 g
Carbohydrates:	5.47 %	35.69 g	17.85 g

CALORIE BREAKDOWN			
Energy (calories):	Total = 1626.00 kcal	Per one serving = 813.00 kcal	
Calorie breakdown:	Percentagewise	Total	Per 1 serving
Protein:	16 %	259.00 kcal	129.50 kcal
Fat:	76 %	1234.00 kcal	617.00 kcal
Carbohydrates:	8 %	133.00 kcal	66.50 kcal

CARBOHYDRATES				
	Per cent of total carbohydrates mass	Per cent of total weight	Total	Per 1 serving
Total Carbohydrates:		5.47 %	35.69 g	17.85 g
Dietary Fiber:	26.62 %	1.46 %	9.50 g	4.75 g
Sugars(net carbs):	63.46 %	**3.47 %**	**22.65 g**	**11.33 g**

39. Coleslaw-Stuffed Keto Wraps

This is a great recipe for anyone who loves to cook.

Ingredients

For coleslaw

- ½ cup of diced green onions
- cups of thinly sliced red cabbage
- 2 tsp of apple cider vinegar
- ¾ cup of mayonnaise
- ¼ tsp of sea salt

Wraps and filling

- 16 collard leaves
- ⅓ cup of packed alfalfa sprouts
- 1 lb of cooked, ground meat

Instructions

- Mix all coleslaw ingredients in a large bowl, ensuring the cabbage and onions are well coated.
- Remove the stems from each collard leaf. (Each leaf should have a missing strip from the base to almost midway up the leaf.)
- Place the first collard leaf on a clean surface.
- Orient the leaf so the base and missing stem strip are further away from you.
- Place a spoonful of coleslaw toward the top edge of the leaf. Put a spoonful of meat on top of that and top with several alfalfa sprouts.
- Roll the top of the leaf over the mixture then begin folding the sides in to prevent the filling from spilling out.
- Continue rolling and try to overlap the edges where the strip is missing.
- When complete, insert 1 or 2 toothpicks to prevent unraveling.
- Repeat with the leftover leaves and filling.
- Divide the wraps into 4 servings of 4 wraps each.

GENERAL			
Servings quantity: 4			
Weight:	Total = 1127.00 g	Per one serving = 281.75 g	
Mass fraction:	Percentagewise	Total	Per 1 serving
Protein:	1.37 %	15.43 g	3.86 g
Fat:	11.15 %	125.64 g	31.41 g
Carbohydrates:	4.18 %	47.16 g	11.79 g

CALORIE BREAKDOWN			
Energy (calories):	Total = 1342.00 kcal	Per one serving = 335.50 kcal	
Calorie breakdown:	Percentagewise	Total	Per 1 serving
Protein:	3 %	40.00 kcal	10.00 kcal
Fat:	84 %	1129.00 kcal	282.25 kcal
Carbohydrates:	13 %	169.00 kcal	42.25 kcal

CARBOHYDRATES				
	Per cent of total carbohydrates mass	Per cent of total weight	Total	Per 1 serving
Total Carbohydrates:		4.18 %	47.16 g	11.79 g
Dietary Fiber:	36.26 %	1.52 %	17.10 g	4.28 g
Sugars(net carbs):	24.47 %	**1.02 %**	**11.54 g**	**2.89 g**

40. Mushroom Omelette

If you have a thing for mushrooms, omelettes, or, better yet, BOTH, try this recipe now!

Ingredients

- ¼ yellow onion, diced
- eggs
- 2-3 mushrooms, sliced
- ⅛ oz of shredded cheddar cheese
- ⅛ oz of butter
- salt and pepper to taste

Instructions

- Crack eggs into a mixing bowl. Add a pinch of salt and pepper.
- Whisk the eggs until smooth.
- Melt butter in a frying pan.
- Pour in the eggs.
- When the bottom has cooked and the top gelled, sprinkle some cheese on top.
- Add mushrooms and onions.
- Carefully lift the edges of one side of the omelette and fold it in half.
- When the omelette has turned golden brown underneath, remove the pan from heat, and slide the omelette onto a plate.

GENERAL			
Servings quantity: 1			
Weight:	Total = 256.00 g	Per one serving = 256.00 g	
Mass fraction:	Percentagewise	Total	Per 1 serving
Protein:	9.58 %	24.53 g	24.53 g
Fat:	16.16 %	41.37 g	41.37 g
Carbohydrates:	2.23 %	5.72 g	5.72 g

CALORIE BREAKDOWN			
Energy (calories):	Total = 491.00 kcal	Per one serving = 491.00 kcal	
Calorie breakdown:	Percentagewise	Total	Per 1 serving
Protein:	21 %	102.00 kcal	102.00 kcal
Fat:	75 %	368.00 kcal	368.00 kcal
Carbohydrates:	4 %	21.00 kcal	21.00 kcal

CARBOHYDRATES				
	Per cent of total carbohydrates mass	Per cent of total weight	Total	Per 1 serving
Total Carbohydrates:		2.23 %	5.72 g	5.72 g
Dietary Fiber:	19.23 %	0.43 %	1.10 g	1.10 g
Sugars(net carbs):	45.98 %	1.03 %	2.63 g	2.63 g

41. Rutabaga Fritters with Avocado

This can be used as a lunch or dinner recipe.

Ingredients

For rutabaga fritters
- eggs
- 1 lb rutabaga
- tbsp coconut flour
- ½ lb of halloumi cheese (grillable or frying cheese)
- oz. butter
- ½ cup turmeric
- 1 tsp salt
- ¼ tsp pepper

For ranch mayonnaise
- 1 cup of mayonnaise
- 1 tbsp of ranch seasoning

For serving
- ⅓ lb of leafy greens, chopped
- avocados, sliced

Instructions
- Preheat oven to 250 °F.
- Make ranch-flavored mayo by combining the mayo and ranch seasoning in a small bowling and mixing.
- Rinse the rutabaga and peel.
- Grate the rutabaga and cheese into a large bowl.
- Add the eggs, coconut flour, salt, pepper, and turmeric. Mix. Let it sit for 5 minutes so the flour is fully saturated.
- Heat butter over medium heat in a large frying pan.
- Ladle the batter into the pan, making a total of 12 patties.
- Fry each patty for 3 to 5 minutes on each side.
- Serve with chopped greens, sliced avocado, and the ranch-flavored mayonnaise.

GENERAL			
Servings quantity: 6			
Weight:	Total = 2253.98 g	Per one serving = 375.66 g	
Mass fraction:	Percentagewise	Total	Per 1 serving
Protein:	4.79 %	107.98 g	18.00 g
Fat:	20.47 %	461.44 g	76.91 g
Carbohydrates:	7.91 %	178.35 g	29.73 g

CALORIE BREAKDOWN			
Energy (calories):	Total = 5113.14 kcal	Per one serving = 852.19 kcal	
Calorie breakdown:	Percentagewise	Total	Per 1 serving
Protein:	11 %	539.03 kcal	89.84 kcal
Fat:	76 %	3894.33 kcal	649.05 kcal
Carbohydrates:	13 %	682.79 kcal	113.80 kcal

CARBOHYDRATES				
	Per cent of total carbohydrates mass	Per cent of total weight	Total	Per 1 serving
Total Carbohydrates:		7.91 %	178.35 g	29.73 g
Dietary Fiber:	51.85 %	4.10 %	92.48 g	15.41 g
Sugars(net carbs):	17.62 %	**1.39 %**	**31.43 g**	**5.24 g**

42. Mushroom Tacos

The addition of mushrooms in this dish makes these tacos scrumptious.

Ingredients

For the portobello mushrooms

- 1 pound of portobello mushrooms
- 6 collard green leaves
- 1 tsp of onion powder
- 1 tsp of ground cumin
- ¼ cup of spicy harissa
- 3 tbsp of olive oil, divided

For the guacamole

- 2 tbsp of chopped red onions
- 2 ripe avocados, medium
- 1 tbsp of chopped cilantro
- 2 tbsp of lemon juice
- 2 tbsp of chopped tomatoes
- A pinch of salt

Instructions

- Remove the stems from the Portobello mushrooms.
- Thoroughly rinse the mushrooms, and dry them.
- In a fresh bowl, add harissa, cumin, 1½ tbsp olive oil, and onion powder.
- Brush the mushrooms with the harissa mixture, ensuring the edges are well-coated.
- Let the mushrooms marinate for 15 minutes.
- While the mushrooms are marinating, you can prepare the guacamole. Cut the avocados in half, and remove the flesh.
- In a bowl, mash the avocados, and add the chopped tomatoes, lemon juice, red onion, salt, and cilantro.
- Remove the stems from the collard greens. Wash the leaves, and place aside.
- When the mushrooms are done marinating, heat 1½ tbsp of olive oil in a skillet over medium heat.
- Now, add the portobello mushrooms to the skillet and cook for 3 minutes.
- Flip them over and cook for 3 more minutes.
- Remove from heat and allow the mushrooms to rest for a couple of minutes before slicing them.
- Fill the collard green leaves with the sliced mushrooms. Add guacamole along with additional chopped tomatoes and cilantro if desired.
- Serve.

GENERAL		
Servings quantity: 6		
Weight:	Total = 1179.00 g	Per one serving = 196.50 g

Mass fraction:	Percentagewise	Total	Per 1 serving
Protein:	2.50 %	29.45 g	4.91 g
Fat:	8.80 %	103.75 g	17.29 g
Carbohydrates:	6.35 %	74.81 g	12.47 g

CALORIE BREAKDOWN			
Energy (calories):	Total = 1235.00 kcal	Per one serving = 205.83 kcal	
Calorie breakdown:	Percentagewise	Total	Per 1 serving
Protein:	7 %	82.00 kcal	13.67 kcal
Fat:	72 %	887.00 kcal	147.83 kcal
Carbohydrates:	21 %	265.00 kcal	44.17 kcal

CARBOHYDRATES				
	Per cent of total carbohydrates mass	Per cent of total weight	Total	Per 1 serving
Total Carbohydrates:		6.35 %	74.81 g	12.47 g
Dietary Fiber:	61.36 %	3.89 %	45.90 g	7.65 g
Sugars(net carbs):	23.17 %	**1.47 %**	**17.33 g**	**2.89 g**

So, now that we are headed to the final meal of the day, let us see some of the best dinner recipes which will ensure that you go to bed happy and healthy.

43. Low Carb Spinach Pie

This meal with a cooking time of only 30 minutes is a great way to have a filling dinner without straying from the diet.

Ingredients

For the crust

- 2 eggs
- ¾ cup of coconut flour
- ½ cup of butter

For the filling

- 4 ounces of crumbled feta
- ½ cup of artichoke hearts, marinated and chopped
- 2 cups of thawed and drained frozen spinach
- Pepper to taste

Instructions

- Preheat the oven to 350 °F.
- Add the thawed spinach and chopped artichoke hearts to a bowl. Press the contents, and drain the excess liquid.
- In a separate bowl, mix the butter and coconut flour until uniform.
- Now, add the two eggs and mix until you have a thick dough that takes the shape of a ball.
- Evenly press the dough in a 9-inch pie pan, and let rest.
- To the drained spinach/artichoke mix, add the feta cheese and pepper. Mix.
- Pour the mixture on to the pie crust dough.
- Bake for 30 minutes.
- Remove from oven and serve.

GENERAL			
Servings quantity: 4			
Weight:	Total = 797.00 g	Per one serving = 199.25 g	
Mass fraction:	Percentagewise	Total	Per 1 serving
Protein:	6.85 %	54.63 g	13.66 g
Fat:	17.39 %	138.62 g	34.66 g
Carbohydrates:	9.81 %	78.19 g	19.55 g

CALORIE BREAKDOWN			
Energy (calories):	Total = 1740.00 kcal	Per one serving = 435.00 kcal	
Calorie breakdown:	Percentagewise	Total	Per 1 serving
Protein:	12 %	206.40 kcal	51.60 kcal

Fat:	70 %	1225.60 kcal	306.40 kcal
Carbohydrates:	18 %	306.00 kcal	76.50 kcal

CARBOHYDRATES			
	Per cent of total carbohydrates mass	Per cent of total weight	Total	Per 1 serving
Total Carbohydrates:		9.81 %	78.19 g	19.55 g
Dietary Fiber:	57.17 %	5.61 %	44.70 g	11.18 g
Sugars(net carbs):	17.76 %	**1.74 %**	**13.89 g**	**3.47 g**

44. Roasted Vegetable and Spinach Pesto

This vegan lasagna-style pesto will certainly be a tasty end to your day. It is sure to satiate your hunger pangs.

Ingredients

- 6 organic large eggs
- 2 medium eggplants
- 10 ounce of fresh spinach
- 1 cup of marinara sauce
- 1½ cup of feta cheese
- ½ cup of parmesan cheese
- 1 cup of mozzarella cheese
- ¼ cup of melted butter
- ½ tsp of salt

Instructions

- Preheat the oven to 400 °F.
- Cut the eggplant into ½ inch slices, and place on a baking sheet.
- Pour the melted butter over the eggplant slices, and season with salt.
- Bake in the oven for 20 minutes. When done cooking, remove from oven and place aside. Lower the oven temperature to 350 °F.
- Blanch the fresh spinach, remembering to place in cold water after cooking. Strain the leaves from the water, and press the spinach to remove any excess liquid.
- Crack one egg and add to a separate bowl. Season with a pinch of salt.
- Pour it into a hot pan that has been greased with melted butter and swirl it around so as to create a very thin layer of cooked egg. Cook it for a minute or so until you feel that the top has firmed.
- Now place it on a plate and repeat the process with the remaining eggs.
- Begin assembling the lasagna by first stacking two of the cooked eggs on a plate.
- Spread 1/3 of the marinara sauce on the top of the stacked eggs, and then add 1/3 of the eggplant slices.
- Now, add ½ of the mozzarella cheese, ½ of the spinach, and ½ of the feta cheese. Then top it with 2 more layers of cooked egg.
- Repeat the layering process, ending with the last 2 layers of cooked egg on top.
- Then add the remaining 1/3 marinara and 1/3 eggplants to top off the lasagna.
- Bake it for 25 minutes.
- Set aside to cool.
- Serve.

GENERAL			
Servings quantity: 8			
Weight:	Total = 2383.00 g	Per one serving = 297.88 g	
Mass fraction:	Percentagewise	Total	Per 1 serving
Protein:	5.52 %	131.56 g	16.45 g
Fat:	7.06 %	168.31 g	21.04 g
Carbohydrates:	4.88 %	116.25 g	14.53 g

CALORIE BREAKDOWN			
Energy (calories):	Total = 2447.00 kcal	Per one serving = 305.88 kcal	
Calorie breakdown:	Percentagewise	Total	Per 1 serving
Protein:	22 %	530.00 kcal	66.25 kcal
Fat:	61 %	1486.00 kcal	185.75 kcal
Carbohydrates:	18 %	430.00 kcal	53.75 kcal

CARBOHYDRATES				
	Per cent of total carbohydrates mass	Per cent of total weight	Total	Per 1 serving
Total Carbohydrates:		4.88 %	116.25 g	14.53 g
Dietary Fiber:	37.59 %	1.83 %	43.70 g	5.46 g
Sugars(net carbs):	56.39 %	**2.75 %**	**65.55 g**	**8.19 g**

45. Crustless Quiche

his can be your go-to recipe when you're in the mood for a light dinner.

Ingredients

- 1½ cups of halved green tomatoes
- 9 large eggs
- 6 oz of mozzarella cheese
- 1 cup of fresh basil
- ½ cup of almond milk, unsweetened
- 4 cloves of garlic, minced
- ¾ tsp of sea salt
- ¼ tsp of black pepper

Instructions

- Preheat the oven to 350 °F.
- In a fresh bowl, add the basil, tomatoes, garlic, and 4 oz mozzarella cheese.
- Mix it well.
- Transfer mixture to a 9" round ceramic pan.
- In a separate bowl, mix together the eggs, milk, salt, and black pepper.
- Add the egg mixture to the ceramic pan.
- Bake it for 30 minutes.
- Remove from oven, and sprinkle the remaining 2 oz mozzarella cheese over the top. Bake it for 15 more minutes.
- Serve.

GENERAL			
Servings quantity: 4			
Weight:	Total = 1051.00 g	Per one serving = 262.75 g	
Mass fraction:	Percentagewise	Total	Per 1 serving
Protein:	9.47 %	99.55 g	24.89 g
Fat:	7.91 %	83.09 g	20.77 g
Carbohydrates:	2.45 %	25.72 g	6.43 g

CALORIE BREAKDOWN			
Energy (calories):	Total = 1258.50 kcal	Per one serving = 314.63 kcal	
Calorie breakdown:	Percentagewise	Total	Per 1 serving
Protein:	34 %	423.38 kcal	105.84 kcal
Fat:	59 %	740.13 kcal	185.03 kcal
Carbohydrates:	7 %	94.00 kcal	23.50 kcal

CARBOHYDRATES				
	Per cent of total carbohydrates mass	Per cent of total weight	Total	Per 1 serving
Total Carbohydrates:		2.45 %	25.72 g	6.43 g
Dietary Fiber:	14.77 %	0.36 %	3.80 g	0.95 g
Sugars(net carbs):	**56.03 %**	**1.37 %**	**14.41 g**	**3.60 g**

46. Low Carb Noodles with Curry Sauce

If you are a noodle kind of person, this recipe is likely to suit you just fine.

Ingredients

For the noodle bowl

- One 0.5 oz. package of Kanten noodles of your choice
- 2 handfuls of mixed greens
- 2 julienned carrots
- 1 diced red bell pepper
- ½ head of roughly chopped cauliflower
- A handful of chopped fresh cilantro

For the creamy curry sauce

- 2 tbsp of apple cider vinegar
- ½ cup of tahini
- ¼ cup of water
- 2 tsp of curry powder
- 2 tbsp of avocado oil
- 1 tsp of ground turmeric
- 1½ tsp of ground coriander
- ¼ tsp of ground ginger
- 1 tsp of ground cumin
- 1 tsp of salt
- ½ tsp of ground black pepper

Instructions

- Prepare the noodles by placing the two sheets of the noodles in the large bowl.
- Heat up 2 cups of water, and remove from heat just before it begins to boil. Add to the bowl of noodles.
- Let noodles sit for 5 minutes. Strain, and let cool in a large bowl.
- Once the noodles have cooled, add cauliflower, cilantro, carrots, and bell pepper to the large bowl.
- Add all of the curry sauce ingredients to a blender, and blend until smooth.
- Pour the blended curry sauce over the vegetable and noodle mixture and toss it thoroughly to coat.
- Place the mixed greens on a serving plate. Top with the noodles, vegetables, and curry sauce mixture.
- Serve.

GENERAL			
Servings quantity: 4			
Weight:	Total = 828.00 g	Per one serving = 207.00 g	
Mass fraction:	Percentagewise	Total	Per 1 serving
Protein:	3.81 %	31.53 g	7.88 g
Fat:	10.73 %	88.85 g	22.21 g
Carbohydrates:	10.37 %	85.89 g	21.47 g

CALORIE BREAKDOWN			
Energy (calories):	Total = 1147.00 kcal	Per one serving = 286.75 kcal	
Calorie breakdown:	Percentagewise	Total	Per 1 serving
Protein:	9 %	102.00 kcal	25.50 kcal
Fat:	66 %	757.00 kcal	189.25 kcal
Carbohydrates:	25 %	282.00 kcal	70.50 kcal

CARBOHYDRATES				
	Per cent of total carbohydrates mass	Per cent of total weight	Total	Per 1 serving
Total Carbohydrates:		10.37 %	85.89 g	21.47 g
Dietary Fiber:	46.69 %	4.84 %	40.10 g	10.03 g
Sugars(net carbs):	19.76 %	**2.05 %**	**16.97 g**	**4.24 g**

47. Keto Crack Slaw

For those who want to keep it a little light, this is a great dinner meal.

Ingredients

- 4 cups of green cabbage, shredded
- 2 tbsp of tamari
- 2 cloves of garlic, minced
- ½ cup chopped macadamia nuts
- 1 tsp of vinegar
- 1 tbsp of sesame oil
- 1 tsp of chili paste
- Sesame seeds and diced green onion, as garnish

Instructions

- Cook cabbage, vinegar, tamari, chili paste, and sesame oil in a pan over medium-low heat.
- Add minced garlic to the pan.
- Cover and cook for about 5 minutes until the cabbage has softened.
- Stir the contents of the pan.
- Now add the nuts and cook for 5 more minutes until they have softened.
- Serve.

Servings quantity: 3			
Weight:	Total = 489.00 g	Per one serving = 163.00 g	
Mass fraction:	Percentagewise	Total	Per 1 serving
Protein:	2.90 %	14.16 g	4.72 g
Fat:	13.25 %	64.81 g	21.60 g
Carbohydrates:	7.16 %	35.03 g	11.68 g

CALORIE BREAKDOWN			
Energy (calories):	Total = 728.00 kcal	Per one serving = 242.67 kcal	
Calorie breakdown:	Percentagewise	Total	Per 1 serving
Protein:	6 %	44.00 kcal	14.67 kcal
Fat:	75 %	549.00 kcal	183.00 kcal
Carbohydrates:	18 %	132.00 kcal	44.00 kcal

CARBOHYDRATES				
	Per cent of total carbohydrates mass	Per cent of total weight	Total	Per 1 serving
Total Carbohydrates:		7.16 %	35.03 g	11.68 g
Dietary Fiber:	43.96 %	3.15 %	15.40 g	5.13 g
Sugars(net carbs):	44.90 %	**3.22 %**	**15.73 g**	**5.24 g**

48. Zucchini Pasta

'or all the pasta lovers out there, this is a great recipe to satisfy your taste buds.

Ingredients

- 2 cup (about 11.5 oz) of cherry tomatoes, halved
- 2 pounds of spiralized zucchini noodles
- 4 cloves of garlic, minced
- ½ cup of fresh basil
- 1 large red onion, thinly sliced
- ¼ cup of extra virgin olive oil
- ½ tsp of crushed red pepper
- Salt and pepper to taste
- 7 oz Shredded parmesan
- ½ cup of shredded parmesan

Instructions

- In a large pot, heat the olive oil over medium.
- Add the garlic and onion to the pan, and cook for about 3 minutes.
- Add the spiralized zucchini noodles to the pot, and season with salt and pepper.
- Cover the pot, and cook for 2 minutes, stirring halfway through.
- Now add tomatoes to the pot and cook for another 3 minutes, making sure to stir every 30 seconds.
- Add fresh basil, crushed red pepper, and parmesan cheese to the pot, and stir.
- Plate the pasta, and garnish with additional basil if desired.
- Serve.

GENERAL			
Servings quantity: 8			
Weight:	Total = 1524.00 g	Per one serving = 190.50 g	
Mass fraction:	Percentagewise	Total	Per 1 serving
Protein:	2.09 %	31.92 g	3.99 g
Fat:	4.52 %	68.94 g	8.62 g
Carbohydrates:	4.02 %	61.22 g	7.65 g

CALORIE BREAKDOWN			
Energy (calories):	Total = 940.00 kcal	Per one serving = 117.50 kcal	
Calorie breakdown:	Percentagewise	Total	Per 1 serving
Protein:	11 %	107.00 kcal	13.38 kcal
Fat:	65 %	607.00 kcal	75.88 kcal
Carbohydrates:	24 %	223.00 kcal	27.88 kcal

CARBOHYDRATES				
	Per cent of total carbohydrates mass	Per cent of total weight	Total	Per 1 serving
Total Carbohydrates:		4.02 %	61.22 g	7.65 g
Dietary Fiber:	26.63 %	1.07 %	16.30 g	2.04 g
Sugars(net carbs):	62.61 %	2.52 %	38.33 g	4.79 g

49. Spaghetti Squash with Basil Pesto

This easy-to-make recipe offers a quick and satisfying meal.

Ingredients for the basil pesto

- ¼ cup pine nuts or cashew nuts
- 1 garlic cloves
- 1 cup fresh basil leaves, packed
- ¼ cup extra virgin olive oil
- ¼ cup freshly grated Parmesan cheese
- 1/8 tsp of black pepper, ground
- 1/8 tsp of salt

Instructions

- Add all of the pesto ingredients to a processor, and blend well. Adding the olive oil slowly, while the processor is running, will help keep the oil from separating and help it emulsify.
- Thus you've got about ¾ cup of basil pesto. You need 3 tbsp of basil pesto for spaghetti squash recipe.

Here are the nutrient facts of pesto:

GENERAL			
Servings quantity: 4 (one serving = 3 tbsp of basil pesto)			
Weight:	Total = 141.00 g	Per one serving = 35.25 g	
Mass fraction:	Percentagewise	Total	Per 1 serving
Protein:	9.02 %	12.72 g	3.18 g
Fat:	59.75 %	84.25 g	21.06 g
Carbohydrates:	6.94 %	9.78 g	2.45 g

CALORIE BREAKDOWN			
Energy (calories):	Total = 821.00 kcal	Per one serving = 205.25 kcal	
Calorie breakdown:	Percentagewise	Total	Per 1 serving
Protein:	6 %	49.00 kcal	12.25 kcal
Fat:	89 %	733.00 kcal	183.25 kcal
Carbohydrates:	5 %	38.00 kcal	9.50 kcal

CARBOHYDRATES				
	Per cent of total carbohydrates mass	Per cent of total weight	Total	Per 1 serving
Total Carbohydrates:		6.94 %	9.78 g	2.45 g
Dietary Fiber:	18.40 %	1.28 %	1.80 g	0.45 g
Sugars(net carbs):	13.70 %	**0.95 %**	**1.34 g**	**0.34 g**

Ingredients for the spaghetti squash

- 1 large (about 5 pounds) spaghetti squash
- 3 tbsp of basil pesto
- 1¼ cups of coarsely grated parmesan cheese, divided
- 2 tbsp of Italian herb blend
- 2 tbsp of olive oil

- Salt and ground pepper to taste

Instructions

- Preheat the oven to 400 °F.
- Now wash the outside of the spaghetti squash and then cut in half lengthwise and scoop out the seeds.
- Cut the ends off the squash and rub the insides with a little olive oil and the Italian herb blend.
- Spray a baking sheet with non-stick cooking spray, and place the spaghetti squash halves on the sheet.
- Bake the squash for about 50 minutes.
- Remove from oven and let cool for a few minutes.
- Using a fork, scrape squash out of skin and place into a bowl.
- Mix the pesto along with the cup of parmesan cheese and then season it with salt and pepper.
- Add the squash in the pesto mixture, pour into the gratin dish, and sprinkle ¼ cup of Parmesan cheese on the top
- Bake it for about 30 minutes.
- Serve.

GENERAL			
Servings quantity: 8			
Weight:	Total = 2019.85 g	Per one serving = 252.48 g	
Mass fraction:	Percentagewise	Total	Per 1 serving
Protein:	2.50 %	50.56 g	6.32 g
Fat:	4.62 %	93.28 g	11.66 g
Carbohydrates:	7.26 %	146.68 g	18.34 g

CALORIE BREAKDOWN			
Energy (calories):	Total = 1537.25 kcal	Per one serving = 192.16 kcal	
Calorie breakdown:	Percentagewise	Total	Per 1 serving
Protein:	13 %	192.25 kcal	24.03 kcal
Fat:	53 %	815.25 kcal	101.91 kcal
Carbohydrates:	34 %	529.50 kcal	66.19 kcal

CARBOHYDRATES				
	Per cent of total carbohydrates mass	Per cent of total weight	Total	Per 1 serving
Total Carbohydrates:		7.26 %	146.68 g	18.34 g
Dietary Fiber:	19.26 %	1.40 %	28.25 g	3.53 g
Sugars(net carbs):	34.44 %	2.50 %	50.52 g	6.32 g

50. Zucchini Ricotta Tart

This light dish surprisingly is quite filling!

Ingredients

For the crust

- 1 tbsp of coconut flour
- ¼ cup of melted butter
- 1¾ cups of almond flour
- ¼ tsp of salt
- ½ tsp of garlic powder

For the filling

- 3 large eggs
- 1 medium-sized (about 5 ounces) zucchini, thinly sliced
- 8 ounces of ricotta
- ¼ cup of whipping cream
- ½ cup of shredded parmesan cheese
- 1 tsp of minced fresh dill
- ½ tsp of salt
- 2 cloves of garlic, minced
- Salt and pepper to taste

Instructions

For the crust

- Preheat the oven to 325 °F. Grease a glass tart pan.
- In a large mixing bowl, mix the coconut flour, almond flour, garlic powder, and salt together.
- Add the melted butter, and mix until the dough is crumbly.
- Press the dough evenly into the greased tart pan, and bake for 15 minutes.
- Let it cool.

For the filling

- Place the zucchini slices in one layer on a towel. Sprinkle with salt.
- Let it sit for 30 minutes.
- Rinse the zucchini slices, and use paper towels to pat them dry.
- In a large bowl, whisk together the whipping cream, ricotta, eggs, dill, garlic, salt, and pepper.
- Stir in most of the zucchini slices, reserving enough for a layer on top of the tart.
- Pour the mixture into the cooled crust.
- Layer the remaining zucchini slices on top, and sprinkle with the parmesan cheese.
- Bake it for an hour.
- Serve.

GENERAL
Servings quantity: 4

Weight:	Total = 877.00 g	Per one serving = 219.25 g	
Mass fraction:	Percentagewise	Total	Per 1 serving
Protein:	12.27 %	107.61 g	26.90 g
Fat:	24.46 %	214.52 g	53.63 g
Carbohydrates:	8.14 %	71.39 g	17.85 g

CALORIE BREAKDOWN			
Energy (calories):	Total = 2532.00 kcal	Per one serving = 633.00 kcal	
Calorie breakdown:	Percentagewise	Total	Per 1 serving
Protein:	21 %	531.66 kcal	132.92 kcal
Fat:	64 %	1630.38 kcal	407.59 kcal
Carbohydrates:	15 %	369.96 kcal	92.49 kcal

CARBOHYDRATES				
	Per cent of total carbohydrates mass	Per cent of total weight	Total	Per 1 serving
Total Carbohydrates:		8.14 %	71.39 g	17.85 g
Dietary Fiber:	36.42 %	2.96 %	26.00 g	6.50 g
Sugars(net carbs):	13.57 %	**1.10 %**	**9.69 g**	**2.42 g**

51. Fettuccini Alfredo

Yet another delicious pasta dish that satisfies and keeps you healthy!

Ingredients

For the pasta

- 1 oz of cream cheese
- 2 eggs
- A pinch of garlic powder
- A pinch of salt
- 1/8 tsp of black pepper

For the sauce

- 1 tbsp of grated parmesan cheese
- 1 oz of Mascarpone cheese
- 1 tbsp of butter

Instructions

For the pasta

- Grease a baking pan with butter. In a blender, add the eggs, garlic powder, cream cheese, salt, and pepper, and blend together.
- Bake at 325 °F for 8 minutes.
- Remove from oven, and let cool for about 5 minutes.
- Using a spatula, remove the sheet of pasta from the baking pan.
- Roll it up, and using a sharp knife, slice it into 1/8 inch slices.
- Unroll and set it aside.

For the sauce

- Add the parmesan cheese, Mascarpone cheese, and butter to a small bowl.
- Microwave it on high for about 30 seconds.
- Stir, and then microwave for an additional 30 seconds.
- Stir until mixture is smooth.
- Add the sliced pasta noodles to the sauce, and toss gently.
- Serve with black pepper to taste.

GENERAL			
Servings quantity: 1			
Weight:	Total = 175.00 g	Per one serving = 175.00 g	
Mass fraction:	Percentagewise	Total	Per 1 serving
Protein:	9.79 %	17.14 g	17.14 g
Fat:	24.60 %	43.05 g	43.05 g
Carbohydrates:	4.75 %	8.32 g	8.32 g

CALORIE BREAKDOWN		
Energy (calories):	Total = 483.00 kcal	Per one serving = 483.00 kcal

Calorie breakdown:	Percentagewise	Total	Per 1 serving
Protein:	16 %	79.00 kcal	79.00 kcal
Fat:	76 %	365.00 kcal	365.00 kcal
Carbohydrates:	8 %	39.00 kcal	39.00 kcal

CARBOHYDRATES				
	Per cent of total carbohydrates mass	Per cent of total weight	Total	Per 1 serving
Total Carbohydrates:		4.75 %	8.32 g	8.32 g
Dietary Fiber:	6.01 %	0.29 %	0.50 g	0.50 g
Sugars(net carbs):	27.28 %	**1.30 %**	**2.27 g**	**2.27 g**

52. Loaded Cauliflower

One of the best low-carb comfort foods ever!

Ingredients
- 1 lb cauliflower florets
- 2 tbsp water
- oz of sour cream
- 2 tbsp of diced chives
- tbsp butter
- 1 cup grated cheddar cheese
- ¼ tsp garlic powder
- salt and pepper to taste

Instructions
- Place cauliflower florets in a bowl along with 2 tbsp water.
- Microwave for 5 to 8 minutes.
- Drain the excess water and let sit uncovered until cool.
- Once cool, blend florets in a food processor until it gets fluffy.
- Add garlic powder, butter, and sour cream. Blend until smooth.
- Place the mashed cauliflower mixture in a fresh bowl, and then add most of the chives.
- Add half of the cheddar cheese and season with salt and pepper. Mix.
- Top the loaded cauliflower with the remaining cheese and chives.
- Microwave for 2 to 3 minutes.

GENERAL			
Servings quantity: 3			
Weight:	Total = 732.00 g	Per one serving = 244.00 g	
Mass fraction:	Percentagewise	Total	Per 1 serving
Protein:	5.55 %	40.60 g	13.53 g
Fat:	11.77 %	86.13 g	28.71 g
Carbohydrates:	4.56 %	33.35 g	11.12 g

CALORIE BREAKDOWN			
Energy (calories):	Total = 1038.00 kcal	Per one serving = 346.00 kcal	
Calorie breakdown:	Percentagewise	Total	Per 1 serving
Protein:	14 %	148.00 kcal	49.33 kcal
Fat:	74 %	767.00 kcal	255.67 kcal
Carbohydrates:	12 %	123.00 kcal	41.00 kcal

CARBOHYDRATES				
	Per cent of total carbohydrates mass	Per cent of total weight	Total	Per 1 serving
Total Carbohydrates:		4.56 %	33.35 g	11.12 g
Dietary Fiber:	28.19 %	1.28 %	9.40 g	3.13 g
Sugars(net carbs):	28.16 %	**1.28 %**	**9.39 g**	**3.13 g**

53. Keto Cheese Shell Taco Cups

Isn't the name cheesy enough to give this recipe a try?

Ingredients

For cheese cups
- 8 slices of your preferred low-carb cheese

For salsa
- 2 diced roma tomatoes
- tbsp of diced red onion
- ½ fresh jalapeno, finely diced
- tbsp cilantro, chopped
- 1 tbsp lime juice

Instructions
- Preheat oven to 375 °F.
- Line a baking sheet with parchment paper and place the cheese slices on it.
- Bake for 5 minutes.
- Remove from oven and let cool slightly.
- Carefully remove the slices and place them in a muffin tin so they take on the cup's shape.
- Let them fully cool.

Making the salsa
- In a fresh bowl, add onions, roma tomatoes, cilantro, jalapenos, and lime juice.
- Mix well.
- Place in the fridge for 30 minutes.
- Fill the cups with salsa filling and enjoy.

GENERAL			
Servings quantity: 2 (4 cheese cups per serving)			
Weight:	Total = 403.00 g	Per one serving = 201.50 g	
Mass fraction:	Percentagewise	Total	Per 1 serving
Protein:	14.01 %	56.45 g	28.23 g
Fat:	16.91 %	68.16 g	34.08 g
Carbohydrates:	2.73 %	10.99 g	5.50 g

CALORIE BREAKDOWN			
Energy (calories):	Total = 876.00 kcal	Per one serving = 438.00 kcal	
Calorie breakdown:	Percentagewise	Total	Per 1 serving
Protein:	27 %	238.00 kcal	119.00 kcal
Fat:	68 %	599.00 kcal	299.50 kcal
Carbohydrates:	4 %	39.00 kcal	19.50 kcal

CARBOHYDRATES				
	Per cent of total carbohydrates mass	Per cent of total weight	Total	Per 1 serving
Total Carbohydrates:		2.73 %	10.99 g	5.50 g
Dietary Fiber:	20.93 %	0.57 %	2.30 g	1.15 g
Sugars(net carbs):	56.60 %	1.54 %	6.22 g	3.11 g

54. Creamy Cauliflower Chowder

Once in a while, it's just nice having soup for dinner, isn't it?

Ingredients
- 1 head of cauliflower cut into small florets
- ¾ cup diced carrots
- ½ cup diced onion
- 1 cup milk
- 1 tbsp butter
- ¼ cup cream cheese
- 5 cloves of garlic, minced
- ½ tsp dried oregano
- 1 tsp freshly ground pepper
- salt to taste
- 1 cup of water
- 1 tbsp of olive oil and 3 oz of shredded cheddar cheese for topping

Instructions
- Heat butter in a soup pot.
- Add onion and garlic and sauté for a few minutes.
- Add cauliflower, carrots, milk, pepper, salt, and oregano.
- Bring this mixture to boil and then reduce heat to a simmer.
- After the cauliflower is tender, remove soup pot from heat and pour the mixture into a blender.
- Blend soup until creamy then pour it back in the pot.
- Add a cup of water along with cream cheese.
- Simmer for 5 to 10 minutes and then turn off heat.
- Top with olive oil and shredded cheddar.

GENERAL			
Servings quantity: 4			
Weight:	Total = 1404.00 g	Per one serving = 351.00 g	
Mass fraction:	Percentagewise	Total	Per 1 serving
Protein:	3.25 %	45.63 g	11.41 g
Fat:	5.96 %	83.71 g	20.93 g
Carbohydrates:	4.59 %	64.44 g	16.11 g

CALORIE BREAKDOWN			
Energy (calories):	Total = 1147.00 kcal	Per one serving = 286.75 kcal	
Calorie breakdown:	Percentagewise	Total	Per 1 serving
Protein:	14 %	162.00 kcal	40.50 kcal
Fat:	65 %	743.00 kcal	185.75 kcal
Carbohydrates:	21 %	240.00 kcal	60.00 kcal

CARBOHYDRATES				
	Per cent of total carbohydrates mass	Per cent of total weight	Total	Per 1 serving
Total Carbohydrates:		4.59 %	64.44 g	16.11 g
Dietary Fiber:	25.14 %	1.15 %	16.20 g	4.05 g
Sugars(net carbs):	**49.97 %**	**2.29 %**	**32.20 g**	**8.05 g**

55. Mint and Feta Fritters

This flavorful dinner recipe can actually serve as a snack as well, depending on your appetite.

Ingredients

- 5 medium-sized courgettes or zucchini (about 5 ounces each)
- 2 medium eggs
- 1.8 oz of feta
- 1 handful of fresh mint
- Butter for frying purposes

Instructions

- Grate the courgette/zucchini and press it with a towel to squeeze out the excess water.
- In a mixing bowl, add the pressed courgette/zucchini gratings, eggs, mint, and feta, and mix well.
- Heat butter on a frying pan.
- Add the egg mixture to the frying pan, and cook until the egg is no longer runny.
- Serve.

GENERAL			
Servings quantity: 4			
Weight:	Total = 961.00 g	Per one serving = 240.25 g	
Mass fraction:	Percentagewise	Total	Per 1 serving
Protein:	2.90 %	27.85 g	6.96 g
Fat:	11.77 %	113.15 g	28.29 g
Carbohydrates:	2.59 %	24.88 g	6.22 g

CALORIE BREAKDOWN			
Energy (calories):	Total = 1191.00 kcal	Per one serving = 297.75 kcal	
Calorie breakdown:	Percentagewise	Total	Per 1 serving
Protein:	9 %	104.00 kcal	26.00 kcal
Fat:	84 %	996.00 kcal	249.00 kcal
Carbohydrates:	8 %	90.00 kcal	22.50 kcal

CARBOHYDRATES				
	Per cent of total carbohydrates mass	Per cent of total weight	Total	Per 1 serving
Total Carbohydrates:		2.59 %	24.88 g	6.22 g
Dietary Fiber:	28.54 %	0.74 %	7.10 g	1.78 g
Sugars(net carbs):	81.19 %	2.10 %	20.20 g	5.05 g

These amazing recipes are all spectacularly compliant with the vegetarian keto diet! We hope you enjoyed many of the recipes from the various categories.

Conversion and Replacements Tables

Equivalents

U.S.	U.S.
16 tablespoons	1 cup
12 tablespoons	3/4 cup
10 tablespoons + 2 teaspoons	2/3 cup
8 tablespoons	1/2 cup
6 tablespoons	3/8 cup
5 tablespoons + 1 teaspoon	1/3 cup
4 tablespoons	1/4 cup
2 tablespoons + 2 teaspoons	1/6 cup
2 tablespoons	1/8 cup
1 tablespoon	1/16 cup
1 pint	2 cups
1 quart	2 pints
1 tablespoon	3 teaspoons
1 cup	48 teaspoons
1 cup	16 tablespoons

Capacity

U.S.	METRIC
1/5 teaspoon	1 ml
1 teaspoon (tsp)	5 ml
1 tablespoon (tbsp)	15 ml
1 fluid oz.	30 ml
1/5 cup	50 ml
1/4 cup	60 ml
1/3 cup	80 ml
3.4 fluid oz.	100 ml
1/2 cup	120 ml
2/3 cup	160 ml
3/4 cup	180 ml
1 cup	240 ml
1 pint (2 cups)	480 ml
1 quart (4 cups)	.95 liter
34 fluid oz.	1 liter
4.2 cups	1 liter
2.1 pints	1 liter
1.06 quarts	1 liter
.26 gallon	1 liter
4 quarts (1 gallon)	3.8 liters

Weight

U.S.	METRIC
.035 ounce	1 gram
0.5 oz.	14 grams
1 oz.	28 grams
1/4 pound (lb)	113 grams
1/3 pound (lb)	151 grams
1/2 pound (lb)	227 grams
1 pound (lb)	454 grams
1.10 pounds (lbs)	500 grams
2.205 pounds (lbs)	1 kilogram
35 oz.	1 kilogram

Keto Flour Nutrition Facts

Serv.size: 1 cup	Energy (calories), kcal	Weight, g	Mass fraction, g				
Type of the flour			Fat	Protein	Carbo-hydrates	Fiber	Sugars (net carbs)
Almond flour	640	112	56	24	24	12	4
Hazelnut flour	720	112	68	16	20	12	4
Coconut flour	480	112	16	16	64	40	8
Chickpea flour	356	92	6.15	20.6	53.19	9.9	9.98
Amaranth flour	440	120	8	16	80	12	0
White Rice flour	578	158	2.24	9.4	126.61	3.8	0.19
Brown Rice flour	574	158	4.39	11.42	120.84	7.3	1.34

Keto Berries Nutrition Facts

Berries	Energy (calories), kcal	Weight, g	Mass fraction, g				
			Fat	Protein	Carbo-hydrates	Fiber	Sugars (net carbs)
Raspberries, frozen, ¼ cup	18.25	35.00	0.23	0.42	4.18	2.28	1.55
Blueberries, frozen, ¼ cup	19.75	38.75	0.25	0.16	4.72	1.05	3.28
Strawberries, frozen, ¼ cup	13.00	37.25	0.04	0.16	3.40	0.78	1.70
Blackberries, frozen, ¼ cup	24.25	37.75	0.16	0.45	5.92	1.90	4.03

Keto-Friendly Vegan Replacements

Ingredients		Serving size	Calories	Carbs	Total sugars in the carbs	Protein	Fat	Note
Egg, whole, middle		1 pcs	63 kcal	0.32 g	0.16 g	5.53 g	4.18 g	
Vegan Keto Replacement	Baking Soda and Vinegar	1 tbsp of baking soda + 1 tbsp of white vinegar	3 kcal	0.01 g	0.01 g	0 g	0 g	A decent egg replacement for fluffier baked goods.
	Silken Tofu	1/4 cup of pureed silken tofu	47 kcal	1.17 g	0.6 g	5.01 g	2.96 g	Silken tofu is a softer form of tofu that perfectly substitutes eggs. It is relatively flavorless but it can make baked goods dense, so it's best used in brownies and some quick breads and cakes.
	Ground Flax Seeds and water	1 tbsp of ground flax seeds + 3 tbsp of water	37 kcal	2.02 g	0.11 g	1.28 g	2.95 g	Finely ground flax makes an excellent binder. It has a nutty flavor that works best in recipes for almond or coconut flour baked goods and pancakes.
	The Neat Egg Natural Vegan Egg Substitute by Neat Foods	1 tbsp of neat egg mix + 2 tbsp of water	25 kcal	4 g	0 g	2 g	0 g	Perfect for baking. Vegan egg substitute that can be used in your favorite recipes as a binding agent in place of real eggs
	The Vegg Baking Mix	1 tsp + 1/4 cup water	10 kcal	1 g	0 g	2 g	0 g	It simulates the function and taste of eggs for baking. This powder works perfectly as a binding agent for all your baking needs. It is great for quiches, cakes, cookies, muffins, challah bread and much more.
	Follow Your Heart's VeganEgg	2 tbps + water	40 kcal	4 g	0 g	1 g	1.5 g	Great for baking cookies, muffins, cakes, and even for cooking up fluffy scrambled eggs and omelets
	The Vegg Tofu Scramble	4 tbsp + water	110 kcal	3 g	0 g	20 g	2 g	This "scrambled egg" mix gives you a high-protein way to enjoy your favorite breakfast foods.
Egg yolk, middle		1 pcs	48 kcal	0.2 g	0.09 g	2.4 g	3.9 g	
Vegan Keto Replacement	The Vegg Vegan Egg Yolk	1/2 tsp + 1/8 cup water	5 kcal	0.5 g	0 g	0.5 g	0 g	This is a 100% plant-based egg yolk replacement. It is great for french toast, dipping, hollandaise, and much more.

Ingredients		Serving size	Calories	Carbs	Total sugars in the carbs	Protein	Fat	Note
Butter		1 tbsp	102 kcal	0.01 g	0.01 g	0.12 g	11.52 g	
Vegan Keto Replacement	Coconut Oil	3/4 tbsp	88 kcal	0 g	0 g	0 g	10.2 g	Coconut oil has a slightly lower melting point than butter and the same smoke point as butter, which makes it a good butter replacement. Coconut oil is great for fat bombs, deserts, and cooking and baking at temperatures under 350 degrees Fahrenheit.
	Olive Oil	3/4 tbsp	89 kcal	0 g	0 g	0 g	10.1 g	You can use olive oil to enhance the flavor and fat content of the many dishes. Just make sure you cook with it at a temperature that is below 405 degrees Fahrenheit, so oil doesn't oxidize and become less healthy.
	Avocado Oil	3/4 tbsp	93 kcal	0 g	0 g	0 g	10.5 g	Avocado oil has the highest smoke point of any other cooking oil (at 520 degrees Fahrenheit), which makes it perfect for cooking, baking, and deep frying.
	Red Palm Oil	3/4 tbsp	90 kcal	0 g	0 g	0 g	11 g	Red palm oil has a mild carrot-like flavor and rich buttery texture. Also, it is a great source of A and E vitamins. Red palm oil is perfect to prepare vegan meats recipes and roast nuts and seeds at temperatures up to 450 degrees Fahrenheit

MCT Oil	3/4 tbsp	90 kcal	0 g	0 g	0 g	10.5 g	MCT oil contains medium-chain fats which are digested easily and sent directly to your liver where they are converted into ketones for fuel. Use this oil in fat bombs, salads, sauces and hot drinks when you need an energy boost.
Vegan Butter	1 tbsp	70-85 kcal	0 g	0 g	0 g	9-10 g	Make sure the vegan butter has no added sugars or hidden carbohydrates and it doesn't contain any hydrogenated oils because these oils increase the risk of heart disease tremendously.

Ingredients		Serving size	Calories	Carbs	Total sugars in the carbs	Protein	Fat	Note
Milk, 2% milkfat		1 cup	122 kcal	12 g	12 g	8 g	5 g	In recipes, you can substitute coconut milk in for regular milk in a 1 to 1 ratio. However, note that there are many varieties of coconut milk which contain different amounts of carbs, sugars, fats and proteins. Just make sure you choose the correct variant of coconut milk.
Milk, 3.25% milkfat		1 cup	149 kcal	12 g	12 g	8 g	8 g	
Vegan Keto Replacement	Coconut Milk	1 cup	45-550 kcal	1-15 g	0-8 g	1-5 g	4-57 g	
Heavy Cream		1 oz	98 kcal	0.8 g	0.8 g	0.6 g	10.5 g	Please, note that there are many varieties of coconut cream which contain different amounts of carbs, sugars, fats and proteins. Just make sure you choose the correct variant. You may have to blend in a bit of water or skim some water out of the container depending on the creaminess of the coconut cream.
Cream, light whipping		1 oz	83 kcal	0.84 g	0.84 g	0.62 g	8.8 g	
Vegan Keto Replacement	Coconut Cream	1 oz	15-95 kcal	1-2 g	0-0.5 g	0-1 g	5-10 g	
Cheese		1 oz	100-115 kcal	0-1 g	0-1 g	6-7 g	8-12 g	Please, note that there are many varieties of vegan cheese which contain different amounts of carbs, sugars, fats and proteins. Just make sure you choose the correct variant. If you want to avoid soy then you can find cashew, coconut or other tree-nut-based cheeses.
Vegan Keto Replacement	Vegan Cheese	1 oz	50-90 kcal	6-10 g	0 g	1-2 g	2-9 g	
Cream Cheese		1 oz	90-110 kcal	0-1 g	0-1 g	1-5 g	5-10 g	Please, note that there are many varieties of vegan cream cheese which contain different amounts of carbs, sugars, fats and proteins. Just make sure you choose the correct variant. If you want to avoid soy then you can find coconut, cashew, and other tree-nut-based cheeses.
Vegan Keto Replacement	Vegan Cream Cheese	1 oz	60-100 kcal	1-2 g	0 g	1-2 g	2-9 g	
Yogurt		1 cup	90-200 kcal	5-50 g	0-8 g	4-20 g	0-5 g	Please, note that there are very many varieties of vegan yogurt, and amounts of carbs, sugars, fats and proteins in these yogurts are very different. Please, make sure you choose the correct variant. You will probably be able to find plain almond, cashew, or coconut milk yogurt. Just make sure it does not contain excess carbs or sugars.
Vegan Keto Replacement	Vegan Yogurt	1 cup	50-400 kcal	2-20 g	0-2 g	4-12 g	0-50 g	
Sour Cream		1 cup	300-500 kcal	10-15 g	0-1 g	7-8 g	25-50 g	Please, note that there are many varieties of vegan sour cream which contain different amounts of carbs, sugars, fats and proteins.

Vegan Keto Replacement	Vegan Sour Cream	1 cup	400-900 kcal	15-25 g	0 g	1-6 g	40-90 g	Just make sure you choose the correct variant of vegan sour cream.

Sweeteners Comparison Table

Sweetener	Type	Energy (calories) per 1 tsp, kcal	Net Carbs per 1 tsp, g	Glycemic Index
Erythritol	Sugar Alcohol	0.8	0.2	0
Stevia	Natural	0.8	0.2	0
Inulin	Natural	6	0.04	0
Allulose	Natural	0.8 - 1.6	0 - 0.2	0
Monk Fruit	Natural	0 - 4	0 - 1	0
Aspartame	Artificial	14.08	3.4	0
Tagatose	Natural	6	1.4	3
Xylitol	Sugar Alcohol	9.6	2.4	13
Maltitol	Sugar Alcohol	10.8	2.68	36
Table Sugar	Processed	15.48	4	63
Sucralose	Artificial	0	0	0-80
Saccharin	Artificial	14.56	3.76	variable

What is the Glycemic Index? This index measures how much your blood sugar is raised by a certain food. Many sweeteners are 0 GI, meaning they don't raise blood sugar. The baseline is glucose, which measures up at 100. Typically you want to use the sweeteners that are lowest in GI, but may find it more beneficial (taste wise) to use a mixture.

For a ketogenic diet, I recommend using erythritol and stevia (or a blend - in combination, they seem to cancel out the aftertaste that each has, and work like a charm) because they are natural, don't cause blood sugar or insulin spikes, and sweeten just perfectly.

Conclusion

We are hopeful that this book has provided keen insight into the vegetarian keto diet and that these recipes will help you enjoy staying on the diet!

These meals and tips should help you make the most of this diet, and soon enough, you will see positive changes in your body and the way you feel. We are very optimistic that when following this diet and including these recipes in your daily meal plan, you will inevitably shed some weight and notice a vast improvement in your health.

So what are you waiting for? Start cooking up some meals and enjoying them right away!

Dear Reader,

Thank you again for purchasing this book!
I hope this book was helpful for you.

And, please, don't forget to receive your free bonus.

I wish you all the best.

Sincerely yours,
Amanda Lee

REMINDER:

Get Your Free Bonus

Keto Diet for Beginners:

Ketogenic Smoothie and Dessert Recipes

Just visit the link or scan QR-code to download it now:

https://goo.gl/qVCCVH

Thanks!

Amanda Lee

Made in the USA
Middletown, DE
12 September 2018